THE
MAKING OF AMERICA
SERIES

NEWARK
NEW JERSEY

These three buildings—Public Service Electric & Gas building, the Raymond Commerce building, and the National Newark and Essex Bank building (from left to right)—were the most important commercial structures in Newark in the 1930s.

THE
MAKING OF AMERICA
SERIES

NEWARK
NEW JERSEY

JEAN-RAE TURNER AND RICHARD T. KOLES

To Pat! Jean-Rae Turner

Richard T. Koles

ARCADIA

ISBN 0-7385-2352-6

Published by Arcadia Publishing,
an imprint of Tempus Publishing, Inc.
2 Cumberland Street
Charleston, SC 29401

Printed in Great Britain.

Library of Congress Catalog Card Number: 2001091017

For all general information contact Arcadia Publishing at:
Telephone 843-853-2070
Fax 843-853-0044
E-Mail sales@arcadiapublishing.com

For customer service and orders:
Toll-Free 1-888-313-2665

Visit us on the Internet at http://www.arcadiapublishing.com

The intersection of Broad and Market Street, known as the Four Corners, was the busiest intersection in the nation in the 1930s.

CONTENTS

ACKNOWLEDGMENTS

Many people have assisted in preparing this book, and we are grateful to all of them. Most of all, we thank Charles F. Cummings, assistant director of the Newark Public Library and Newark City Historian, and his staff in the New Jersey Information Center, including Robert Blackwell, Valerie Austin, James Osbourn, Ralph Tohlin, and Willis Taylor, for helping us find the items we needed.

We give special thanks to Don Davidson, owner of New Jersey Newsphotos, for permitting us to use photos from his collection and for using his darkroom and office equipment until December 1999. Without them, we would have been lost.

We especially thank Barbara Moss, who has assisted us in attempting to grasp the mysteries of computer operation and those who donated photographs and material, including Edna Anselm, Beth Israel Medical Center, Nancy Campbell, Doris Curtin Cox, Cheryl Erenberg, Alma Flagg, Patricia Foley, Shirley Frazer, William Gural, Mary Hill, Doris and Irwin Honigfeld, the members and staff of the Jewish Historical Society at Metro West, Mary Keller, Robert Kyber, Gerald McCrea, the New Jersey Symphony Orchestra staff, Russell Ogden, Patricia Pagnetti, Victor Parsonnet, Herman and Courtney Sorey, Howard Wiseman, Helen Whiting, James Wright and his mother, Josephine Wright, Lauren Yeats, Michael Yesenko, and most of all, Elaine Smith, for giving us the photographs taken by her husband, Edward.

INTRODUCTION

Newark, New Jersey, means many places to different people. It is "Swing City" to Barbara Kukla, Newark section editor of the *Star Ledger*, New Jersey's largest newspaper. Charles F. Cummings, Newark City historian and assistant director of the Newark Public Library in charge of special collections, calls it "the last Puritan theocracy in New Jersey," or the city with the most outstanding Art Deco architecture. The nation's media calls it the place where there were riots in the hot summer of 1967, forgetting that civil disturbances occurred in cities across the nation. They also have called it the car theft capital of the nation, and one paper termed it the murder capital of the country.

To the colonists, it was the future Zion, a holy land, where life would be as close to heaven as possible. To the colonial residents, the British army, and their mercenaries, it was the place to drink good intoxicating "Jersey lightning," better known as hard cider.

Census takers find it New Jersey's largest city. Essex County has kept it as its county seat. Several federal agencies and corporations have selected it for offices. Thousands of students who attend the medical school, two law schools, two colleges, and one community college call it a college town.

Their parents think of Newark as the place to earn their livings in the insurance, banking, and assorted businesses or at the Newark International Airport, Port Newark, warehousing, 5 hospitals, 70 public, private, and parochial schools, and more than 100 factories. Law firms are housed in the new Law Center and several state offices are scattered around the city in refurbished buildings.

Senior citizens recall it as a shopping haven with places for pleasant lunches and festive dinners as well as the center of entertainment, especially on Saturday nights for Broadway previews, motion picture shows, concerts, or dancing. They remember also the hundred or so beautiful churches and synagogues with their many organizations conducting socials or fund-raisers.

The older citizens remember singing in the Festival Chorus, a church choir, or a saenger society at a German song fest; they remember belonging to clubs such as the Rotary, the Essex, the Contemporary, the A. Kempis, the No Nothing, which became the Progress Club. They talk about their experiences learning to swim at the three Ys or seeing future Broadway and Hollywood greats hone their talents at Fuld Hall at the YM-YWHA. Most of all, they talk about strolling in the parks, learning to play tennis, participating in a softball game, watching trotting races at Weequahic Park, enjoying picnics on the grass in the shade of huge trees, visiting the free Newark Museum to see exhibits or hear a lecture, and exploring the Newark Public Library, where a whole world of books was theirs for the borrowing.

Settled on May 18, 1666, by Puritans from Milford in Connecticut accompanied by Captain Robert Treat, Newark covered all of present-day Essex County and parts of Passaic, Morris, Somerset, Bergen, and Union Counties. High Street, now Martin Luther King Jr. Boulevard, was considered to be the frontier for more than 100 years.

When the various counties were formed, Essex County was reduced to some 139.52 square miles, of which 2.42 square miles were water. Twenty-one new municipalities were formed as people settled north of Second River and west of the First and Second Mountains. They include Orange in 1808; Bloomfield, 1812; Livingston, 1813; Belleville, 1839; Irvington, 1852; Millburn, 1857; South Orange, 1861; East Orange, 1863; Montclair, 1868; Caldwell, 1892; Glen Ridge, 1895; North Caldwell, 1898; West Orange, 1900; Essex Fells, 1902; Nutley, 1902; West Caldwell, 1904; Verona, 1907; Cedar Grove, 1908; Roseland, 1908; Maplewood, 1920; and Fairfield, 1964. As a result of these new villages and towns, Newark covers only 24.4 square miles.

The land extended from Newark Bay up the Passaic River to a crossing at Aquackanonk to the Orange or Watchung Mountains to Divident Hill. It contained swampy marshes, meadowlands with the famous Jersey grasses, and gentle hills covered with oak, maple, chestnut, elm, and other varieties of trees and bushes with blue or blackberries.

The Passaic River and the streams flowing into it had an abundance of fish and waterfowl such as geese and ducks. Wild turkeys flew overhead, and wild animals such as foxes, wolves, raccoons, beavers, and bears roamed the woods. Each spring there were shad runs, and oysters and clams could be found in the mud along the river. There was ample clear water for drinking, washing, cooking, and gardening.

The river provided easy transportation. Shallow draft boats called periaugers were used to go up the streams such as the Elizabethtown River, Bound Creek, and Second River. At least five wharves were built along the Passaic River and there were two docks on Bound Creek near the Road to Elizabethtown opposite each other—one was for Elizabethtown and the other for Newark Town.

The settlers were very much alone except for neighboring Elizabethtown. There were few American Indian tribes. Some historians estimate that there were only 5,000 when the first white settlers came to New Jersey. The Newark settlers

Early Newark proprietor Julius Lewitt stands in front of his grocery store on South Orange Avenue with his family c. 1895.

had no trouble with them after they established homes and towns. Unfortunately, these American Indians caught the European diseases carried by the newcomers and many died. The Dutch, who controlled New Amsterdam, had a few settlements along the Hudson and Raritan Rivers, but they were mostly interested in fur trading. The trails the Dutch followed were begun by the Indians and animals before them.

Early Newark was an agrarian society. A few of the first citizens were artisans and conducted workshops in their homes. There were fewer than 1,000 persons in Newark at the close of the Revolutionary War. Cottage industries continued to thrive until Seth Boyden arrived in 1815 and began forming companies, inventing products, selling companies, and going on to another project. Historian Charles F. Cummings calls him "the Father of Newark Industry."

Already recognized for its cider that was sent to ports along the American coast, Newark became known for its shoes and boots, beer, trunks, carriages, wagons, varnish, paint, harnesses, saddles, jewelry, hats, Celluloid, electrical instruments, thread, ships, sterling silver objects, machinery, chemicals, and hundreds of other products. Support services such as banks and insurance companies were formed by early businessmen to assist them, making Newark the financial center of New Jersey.

The factories attracted immigrants, and these new Americans needed services such as schools, hospitals, and churches, which were built for and by them. At first, factory owners lived adjacent to their factories. Later, they moved to

9

mansions on High Street, Lincoln, Washington, or Military Parks. Then, they moved to the suburban sections of the city like Forest Hill, Clinton Hill, Weequahic, Roseville, or Vailsburg. After World War I, they began moving to Maplewood, Millburn (Short Hills), and South Orange. Since World War II, they began migrating also to West Orange, Livingston, and Roseland, as well as Morris, Union, and Somerset Counties.

Meanwhile, the factories were becoming outmoded and the products old-fashioned. These early businessmen either moved to the suburbs for more land, relocated to the Southern states for cheaper labor, or simply closed. Newark's old factories when empty were vandalized, burned by arsonists, or inhabited by drug addicts. Shopping malls in the countryside replaced many of the city stores.

While many people have fled the city in fear because of the past riot, some have returned to live and to enjoy Newark's concert halls, museum, library, and churches. Hundreds leave their suburban neighborhoods daily to attend programs at the Newark Museum, Newark Public Library, and New Jersey Performing Arts Center. Others return to work in public and private social agencies to assist the people who remain in Newark.

The *Making of America: Newark, New Jersey* will remember both the good and the bad and show how one community is striving to solve the problems of urbanization that plagues all of America's densely populated cities.

Street repairs meant the removal of cobblestones from Market Street near Broad Street as automobiles replaced horse-drawn wagons.

FOREWORD

This year marks the 355th anniversary of Newark, first as a township and then as a city, making it the third oldest major American city following Boston and New York. This new graphic history of Newark shares some of its contributions to the American experience.

In many ways Newark was the first stop in America's march west from the Atlantic to the Pacific. Located only 9 miles west of Manhattan, the center of downtown Newark commands a view of New York's Wall Street and Midtown. In a recent exhibition and lecture series in France, noted author and native son Philip Roth described Newark as separated from New York by meadows and three great rivers: the Hudson, Hackensack, and Passaic.

While Newark grew independently in its own right, at the same time it is a part of the nation's largest metropolitan complex. But it is not just a suburb. The immigrants who came to settle and to build up its industry and transportation network all contributed locally and in many instances moved on into America's hinterlands.

Beginning as a seventeenth-century Puritan experiment, developing from simple craft industries to great industrial complexes by the time of the Civil War, riding the roller coaster of twentieth-century American history with its wars, depressions, Prohibition, and riots, Newark managed each time to land on its feet to begin a new era. Its recent revival, which may have begun in the New Newark Movement of the 1950s and continued into the Renaissance movement of the twenty-first century, shows the city's remarkable resiliency. Today, Newark continues to offer a strong industrial and commercial base, excellent transportation, an impressive "cultureplex," and advances in high technology. These are some of the themes that authors Jean-Rae Turner and Richard T. Koles have shown in their study of Newark.

—Charles F. Cummings

11

1. THE TOWN ON THE PASSAIC

In the mid-1600s, the English settlers on the eastern end of Long Island and on the Long Island Sound in Milford, Branford, and Guilford wanted to move to the attractive land along the Passaic River or the Arthur Kill. They sent delegations to Dutch Governor Peter Stuyvesant in New Amsterdam (New York) for permission, and like many politicians of any era, Governor Stuyvesant indicated neither a "no" nor a "yes."

Before they could ask again, Captain (and later governor) Richard Nicolls sailed into New Amsterdam and captured it for the English. The colonists immediately went to him with their request to settle this new land. Since Nicolls had been directed by King Charles II of England to settle the land, it was an easy decision.

Four families from the eastern end of Long Island arrived in October 1664 to claim the land. They also visited Mattano, a Lenape Indian on Staten Island, and paid him for the land. These intrepid early Americans sailed 2.5 miles up the creek (later called the Elizabeth River) to the head of tide for their settlement. The site became the center of the hamlet, with a courthouse and church constructed, and later a library.

Governor Nicolls gave these first families their rights as Englishmen. These rights included religious freedom, as long as it was Protestant, free choice of officers, entitlement to town lots, the right to vote, and the power to hold office. The property tax was delayed five years. Sixty-five men from Long Island were stockholders when Captain Philip Carteret arrived in August 1665.

Many of the deeds for property used the stone bridge as a landmark in their descriptions of property. John Ogden, who was probably the oldest man in the new settlement, erected two mills near the bridge: the first for cutting lumber and the second for grinding grain. Most of the settlers were natives of Massachusetts or the New Haven colonies.

The settlers, who called themselves the Associates, drew lots for their future home sites. Each one received a portion of land in town, meadowland, and

This statue of two pilgrims is one of four done by Gutzon Borglum in Newark. Called the First Landing Party of the Founders of Newark, *it was unveiled in 1916, near the original landing on Saybrook Place, as part of the 250th anniversary of the settlement of Newark. It was moved to the grounds of the New Jersey Performing Arts Center in 1997 and is located just above McCarter Highway.*

upland. They were busy constructing houses and barns, tending their crops, and attempting to turn the wilderness into happy and safe homes when Captain (and later governor) Philip Carteret waded ashore in August 1665.

He joined the Associates, shouldered a hoe, and drew for land like the other Associates. Captain Carteret represented his cousins, Sir George and Lady Elizabeth Carteret of the Isle of Jersey, the proprietors of the land, and he named the area New Jersey for his home island and the hamlet Elizabethtown for Lady Elizabeth. James, Duke of York, later King James II, deeded the land to Sir George and John Lord Berkeley in payment for debts he owed them. King James II, in turn, had received the land from his brother, King Charles II. John Lord Berkeley took West Jersey.

Governor Carteret gave the settlers the Concessions and Agreements, which conferred upon the people the rights of freemen in England. Unlike Governor Nicolls's grant, however, the agreements included quitrents (payments) of a half-penny an acre of land and a peppercorn, a dried hot pepper, to the Proprietors. The colonists refused to pay, for they felt that they owned the land and they lacked

This 40-foot-long mural by C.Y. Turner depicts the landing of the Puritans at the Landing Place on the Passaic River. John Ward (the turner in the center) is seen assisting future wife, Elizabeth Swaine, ashore.

hard money—most of their trade was done by barter. The two groups, Associates and Proprietors, claimed ownership of the land, and this alleged dual ownership would cause problems of land titles until the Revolutionary War.

One of the first visitors that Governor Carteret received after his arrival was the delegation from Milford, Branford, and Guilford in the New Haven Colony. The members of the delegation wanted land on which to settle. They were unhappy about the charter from King Charles II merging the New Haven and Connecticut colonies and they were unhappy about the attitude of the Connecticut colonists toward religion.

The New Haven people called them the Half Way Covenant because they were willing to be baptized and were willing to have their children baptized, but they failed to display any evidence of inner spirituality. The New Haven settlers wanted strict observance of the Puritan ideals, and Governor Carteret was the answer to their prayers. He granted them about half of the Elizabethtown area.

Captain Robert Treat sailed 4 miles up the Passaic River from the bay on May 18, 1666, with 30 families from Milford in several small boats loaded with children, household goods, and farm animals. The Lenape Indians prevented Treat's party from landing and demanded payment.

Captain Treat hurried to Elizabethtown, where Governor Carteret, according to many historians, admitted his failure to inform the Lenapes of the party's intentions. Captain Treat met with the Lenape tribe, who demanded 50 double hands of powder, 100 bars of lead, 20 axes, 20 coats, 10 guns, 20 pistols, 10 kettles, 10 swords, 4 blankets, 50 knives, 20 hoes, 2 ankers of liquor, and 3 trooper's coats. Treat paid, and several years later, this parcel was enlarged with additional payments.

The early settlers called their new home, New Milford, for their old one near New Haven. This name was changed to Newark when Reverend Abraham Pierson, the spiritual advisor from Branford, arrived with another group of settlers in 1667. As a tribute to Reverend Pierson's home, Newark-On-Trent, England, the place was renamed Newark.

The people that accompanied Reverend Pierson settled southwest of the hamlet in a place called Connecticut Farms, now part of Union Township. In many respects, these people could be considered the first to move out of Newark. Presently, the football team at Union High School is called the Connecticut Farmers in remembrance of these early settlers.

The early Newarkers were stricter than their relatives and friends in Elizabethtown, for they believed that they were especially chosen by God and all their actions must be determined by the Bible. Only church members could vote or hold office before 1677, and there was only one church, the Congregational Church. Attendance was compulsory. Unlike Elizabethtown, which at first lacked a pastor, Newark was a theocracy. Reverend Pierson had helped found the settlement and later passed his leadership and ministry to his son, Reverend Abraham Pierson Jr. Newark, in many ways, was the last Puritan settlement in New Jersey.

The first General Assembly of New Jersey met at Elizabethtown on May 26, 1668. Each of the five settlements sent two representatives. The delegates from Newark were Captain Treat and Samuel Swaine. Others were from the settlements at Bergen, Elizabethtown, Woodbridge, Middletown, and Shrewsbury. The first four counties in East New Jersey were formed as Essex County, containing both Newark and Elizabethtown; Bergen County; Middlesex County with Woodbridge; and Monmouth County with Middletown and Shrewsbury. Seventeen additional counties have been formed since.

This monument to Reverend Abraham Pierson, a Congregational minister, is located at Yale University in New Haven, Connecticut. Reverend Pierson is responsible for renaming Newark in honor of his native town, Newark-On-Trent, in England.

Before the church with its bell tower was erected, early settlers were called to church services, municipal meetings, and emergencies such as fires by a drummer. The structure seen here is an artist's impression of the appearance of the first church built in Newark, on the west side of Broad Street. The third church building, constructed after the second burned during the war, is still standing.

Life for Governor Carteret was difficult. He lost his seat as governor twice. On the first occasion, James Carteret, son of Sir George Carteret, arrived and sided with the Associates, who elected him governor. Philip Carteret sailed to England to protest.

The British and Dutch began fighting again, and on July 30, 1673, the Dutch recaptured New York and demanded that all of the English colonists swear allegiance to them; many did. The war between Holland and England ended February 9, 1674, with a Dutch defeat. Governor Carteret returned November 6, 1674, restoring the Proprietary government.

However, his problems were far from being over. Governor Edmund Andros felt that he had jurisdiction over New Jersey because he was appointed governor of New York by the Duke of York. Carteret, in a meeting with Andros in an open field in Elizabethtown, disputed the claim. Governor Andros signed a warrant for Carteret's arrest and on May 1, 1680, his deputies sailed up the Elizabethtown River, seized Carteret in his night clothes at his home, and jailed him. Governor Carteret pleaded innocent to all charges, and a jury found him innocent. Governor Andros disputed the verdict and two more trials were conducted with the same results. Carteret was eventually released.

When he returned to Elizabethtown, he married Elizabeth Smith Lawrence, a widow from Long Island, in April 1681. Interestingly, Elizabeth had Carteret sign a prenuptial agreement, probably one of the first in the American colonies, stating that he would not have any rights of possession to the land she had inherited from William Lawrence for her sons. They were married only a year when Philip died. After Carteret's death, she married Richard Townley and several of their descendants still live in New Jersey.

The early settlers planned their community. Unlike other colonial villages, Newark Town had and still has a 132-foot-wide Broad Street and Market Street that crossed each other at the town's center, the Four Corners, now on the National Register of Historic Places. The other streets or lanes were like typical colonial streets, just wide enough for two wagons to pass each other.

The early citizens of the town signed the Fundamental Agreement on June 24, 1667, on how the town would be governed and conducted. They drew for 6-acre lots. Captain Treat and Reverend Pierson received 2 additional acres as did fishermen for their boats on the river. All recipients of land were required to build a house on that land and reside in it for two years before selling it. They also were directed by local mandate to dig a drainage ditch in front of their property.

Trees were cleared from the land. Timber was needed for dwellings, barns, and out buildings. Logs were prepared for the fireplaces to heat the houses and to cook the food. The seeds they had carried with them from their homes in Milford, Guilford, and Branford were planted for kitchen gardens and apple orchards. Apples were not native to this country. The cider made from them was sold in the other colonies and was carried to them on the periaugers, shallow draft boats that could sail up the streams.

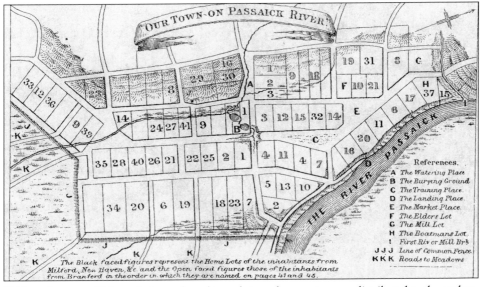

This early map of Newark shows how house lots and property were distributed to the settlers.

The Sydenham House, on Old Bloomfield Road near Heller Parkway, was built c. 1710 for John and Susannah Sydenham in the present Forest Hill section. It is the oldest private residence still standing in the city.

While some of the settlers had springs on their own property or dug wells, water was abundant in the Passaic River. The Frog Pond near Four Corners usually was used by local farmers for livestock. Silver Lake, Paterson's Pond, and the numerous streams such as First, Second, and Third Rivers, Bound Creek, Branch Creek, and the Elizabeth River were also used by many as a local water supply.

The land rose gently from 3 feet above the Passaic River to 258 feet above sea level near Second River or at the source for First River. Today, they are the Newark-Belleville line and Martin Luther King Boulevard (High Street), respectively. Second River, or Mill Creek North of the hamlet, became the future boundary between Newark and Belleville. A stone bridge crossed it and a bridge still stands today on Broadway in Newark to Washington Avenue in Belleville. Unlike the bridge in Elizabethtown, which is mentioned in many deeds, this bridge went unnoticed in local legal notices and documents.

As the families grew and more colonists arrived, people began to move beyond First and Second Mountains seeking land for farms. After they established their homes, they realized that attending church services in Newark was a long trip. One of these groups, called the Mountain Society in present West Orange, established its own church about 1718. This was the beginning of the subdivision of Newark.

About the same time that the Mountain Society decided it would continue to be a Congregational Church, Reverend Jonathan Dickinson, pastor of the church in Elizabethtown, joined the Presbytery of Philadelphia. His action caused the church in Newark Town to follow suit. Presbyterian churches replaced the Congregational churches, and most of the present-day Congregational churches in New Jersey were organized in the late nineteenth century. The Presbytery of New Jersey was formed in 1733. The Mountain Society later became the First Presbyterian Church of Orange.

A Dutch Reformed Church began in the future Belleville during this period. It appears to have been established by Dutch who had moved into the area. Like the Presbyterian and Congregational churches, it was part of the reformed tradition and there were no problems of note among the churches. The First Dutch Reformed Church at 169 1/2 Market Street was formed in 1833, long after the Belleville church. Three other Dutch Reformed Churches were organized in Newark in the nineteenth century. Only the North Reformed Church, opposite Washington Park, is in use today.

The churchgoers were elated in 1739 by George Whitefield, who arrived on a preaching tour encouraging the Great Awakening, a spiritual movement that was sweeping the colonies. Whitefield took the people who attended his services to task for their apathy in religious matters. The people in Newark responded to his evangelism with a great outburst of religious emotion.

The Plume farmhouse was erected in 1710. When the House of Prayer, an Episcopal church, was erected in 1850, this residence served as the rectory. Railroad and highway construction have threatened the house and church, now in the shadow of Route 280 and the former Erie-Lackawanna Railroad.

An outgrowth of Whitefield's visit was the desire by the Presbyterian ministers in New Jersey for a college to train young men as ministers to replace Yale College in New Haven. Reverend Jonathan Dickinson and Reverend Aaron Burr Sr., pastor of the Newark church, applied for and were given a charter in 1746 for the College of New Jersey, now Princeton University.

The school was organized in Elizabethtown, but moved to Newark the following year, after Reverend Dickinson's death and Reverend Burr's succession as president. The college was moved to the new Nassau Hall in Princeton in 1756 by Reverend Burr, and the name Nassau was suggested by Governor Jonathan Belcher of Elizabethtown in honor of William III, Prince of Orange.

Unfortunately, Reverend Burr died the next year. Despite the fact that he was an outstanding pastor and college president, he usually is remembered best as the father of Aaron Burr Jr., a vice-president of the United States who killed Alexander Hamilton in a duel at Weehawken.

Although Newark's residents were noted for their strict religious practices, there were significant dissensions that had an impact on the community. Josiah Ogden, a son of Elizabeth Swaine Ward Ogden and David Ogden, took his family and farmhands into his hay field on a Sunday morning to remove his dried, cut wheat. According to local legend, Ogden acted after several days of rain had soaked the wheat. When it had dried, he wanted to store it in his hay loft so that it wouldn't rot and become waste.

This is an artist's depiction of Josiah Ogden and his helpers working on the Sabbath as disapproving fellow Presbyterians pass by.

Trinity Episcopal Church was organized in 1743 after meeting in homes for several years. Trinity became the seat of the Diocese of Newark for the Anglican churches.

His fellow Presbyterians saw him as they were on their way to church. After the services, a group arrived at his field and scolded him for working on the Sabbath. Ogden was hurt and embarrassed. He and others who liked the Anglican service began to meet in each other's homes until a building could be erected adjacent to the training place. The tower of this original building still stands. The church now is Trinity-St. Phillips Episcopal Cathedral, and it is the seat of the Episcopal Diocese of Newark.

A third denomination, the Baptists, organized a church on the road to Elizabethtown (Elizabeth Avenue) on April 16, 1769, as the Lyons Farms Baptist Church. Unlike the other churches where the people came up the rivers, this church was formed by a group that came overland from Scotch Plains. The Scotch Plains Baptist Church, in turn, was organized on September 8, 1747, by the Piscataway Baptist Church, founded in 1707. It became the founding church of most of the Baptist churches in Essex County.

The fourth denomination, the Methodists, came into the county at the end of the eighteenth century with meetings both in Elizabethtown and Newark Town. The Newark congregation started in a bark mill near the future Halsey Street Methodist Episcopal Church.

The Lyons Farms Baptist Church was the mother of most of the Baptist churches in Newark. This one became the Calvary Gospel Church in 1964, and it also operates a day school.

The Puritanism of the early settlers, however, continued to have a strong hold on the residents and would continue to do so until well into the nineteenth and early twentieth centuries. Only necessary work was to be performed on the Sabbath, such as feeding animals, cow milking, or meal preparing. Reading was permitted on Sundays, but entertainments such as the movies, dancing, and card playing were prohibited for many years, as were sewing or lawn mowing. Concerts were approved, but theater-going was not.

Protestant churches thrived and multiplied in the eighteenth and nineteenth centuries. Although there were Roman Catholics among the colonists, there were too few to start a church until 1826. Those people who wished to attend Mass traveled into New York City. Some Jews had settled in the colonies during the eighteenth century with the Germans, but no Jewish citizens were recorded in Newark until the 1840s. Newark would continue to be mainly Protestant through the nineteenth century. The Zion the early settlers sought was still to be found and many would continue to seek it.

2. To Protect Our Soil

From the beginning of America, relations between the settlers and the Proprietors were troublesome. The settlers, who were supposed to pay a peppercorn as well as quitrents to the Proprietors, refused and never paid it. There were questions over land titles that like the quitrents and peppercorn were still unsolved when the Revolutionary War began.

The Crown prohibited the purchase of land from the Native Americans, for it claimed that the Crown owned all property. Instead, the colonists were ordered to pay the Proprietors for their land. The colonists drew up a new deed and had the descendants of the original Indians sign it. Several of the townspeople were arrested by the Proprietary government, and a mob formed and forcibly released the prisoners. Some time later, after several more incidents, Amos Roberts was arrested and charged with high treason for being the leader of the rioters. A large number of his friends at "early candle light" raided the jail and freed him.

Probably more problematic than the land controversies was the British restriction on trade and manufacturing by the colonists. At least two lodes of copper were found in the Town of Newark. Under colonial law, the freshly mined copper had to be sent to England for refining. Several illegal forges were hidden in the woods so that the work could be done in New Jersey.

Ships also could only trade along the coast of the American colonies or with England. They were prohibited from trading with islands in the Caribbean or with European countries. The shipmasters wanted the right to trade where they desired to without having to go to England first.

The last straw came when England adopted the Stamp Act, taxing all legal documents. An assembly called at Perth Amboy by Robert Ogden of Elizabethtown condemned the Stamp Act as unconstitutional and destructive to the liberties of Americans. Under the British law, no business could be conducted without the taxed stamps on the documents. Finally, lawyers and public officials decided to issue legal papers without the stamps. The British Parliament adopted

From the time that Newark was settled until after the Civil War, the training place on Broad Street was used to drill the militia and army recruits. After the Civil War, it became Military Park. The market place to the north became Washington Park, and a common on Broad Street at Clinton Avenue, sometimes called South Park, was renamed in honor of President Abraham Lincoln.

the Townshend Acts, setting duties on all goods not imported from Britain. The colonists objected to these also and all duties, except the tax on tea, were repealed. The colonists, however, decided not to purchase anything on the list.

Parliament next adopted a measure outlawing the use of paper money as legal tender in the colonies. A bill in New Jersey that would have permitted its use was disallowed by British authorities. Meanwhile, Parliament adopted the Coercive Acts, closing the Port of Boston and demanding that citizens of Boston and the Massachusetts Colony pay for the tea dumped into the harbor during the Boston Tea Party in 1773.

The response in the colonies was to call a meeting of the Continental Congress to consider the crisis. The people in the Town of Newark at a meeting of Essex County representatives decided a provincial convention should be conducted at New Brunswick. William Peartree Smith, then of Elizabethtown, later of Newark, was selected as the head of the committee of correspondence to keep the delegates informed. A liberty pole was erected on the training ground, the future Military Park, by the more combative members of the community, who called themselves the Sons of Liberty. Men began training on the green.

The colonists were divided long before shots were fired on April 19, 1775, in Massachusetts and the British Navy blocked the Port of Boston. Some of the people in Newark feared that their port would be blocked by British warships too. The Dutch residents took little interest in the dispute, figuring it was just an argument between the English in the colonies and the English in England. The Quakers were noncombatants, and the rest of the colonists supported the Crown.

On June 17, 1775, the British attacked and defeated the Continental troops on Breed's Hill, near Bunker Hill in Boston, but they suffered heavy casualties. The Continental Congress selected George Washington to lead the Continental troops, and he passed through Newark with Major Generals Charles Lee and Philip Schuyler. Reverend Dr. Alexander Macwhorter of the Presbyterian Church, Newark officials, and representatives of the New York Provincial Congress greeted General Washington at Newark.

The route he was traveling to New York City was changed because it was feared that there were too many Loyalists at Paulus Hook (Jersey City). The party instead rode to Hoboken and crossed the Hudson River there, with six accompanying companies of Essex County Minute Men. These companies later were merged with the militia. Each man supplied his own bullets, gun or musket, and uniform. An order was issued by the Continental leaders not to kill or eat sheep because their wool was needed for clothing.

The Revolutionary War in New Jersey was known as "the Presbyterian War," because of the number of Presbyterian pastors and congregations that participated in it. Reverend John Witherspoon of Princeton, president of the College of New Jersey, was one of the signers of the Declaration of Independence. Other signers were Richard Stockton, an attorney of Princeton; Abraham Clark of

The statue of General George Washington and his horse by J. Massey Rhind (1912) in Washington Park is dwarfed by an assortment of office buildings across the street.

Reverend Dr. Alexander Macwhorter, pastor of the First Presbyterian Church in Newark from 1759 to 1807, was a confidant of General George Washington and a leader for the Revolutionary cause in Newark.

Elizabethtown, who was known as "the Poor Man's Lawyer"; John Hart, a farmer from Hopewell; and Francis Hopkinson of Bordentown, New Jersey's first composer. Reverend James Caldwell, pastor of the Presbyterian Church in Elizabethtown, served as chaplain of Colonel Elias Dayton's battalion in Elizabethtown, while Reverend Dr. Alexander Macwhorter, pastor of Newark's Presbyterian church, became chaplain of General Henry Knox's brigade at White Plains and frequently consulted with General Washington.

Oddly enough, the first constitution of the new State of New Jersey was adopted by the Provincial Congress on July 2, 1776, two days before the adoption of the Declaration of Independence, announcing the colony's freedom from England. New Jersey approved the Declaration on July 8, 1776. New Jersey's first constitution granted the franchise to all persons if they possessed 50 pounds.

Early on June 29, 1776, observers on Divident Hill and other lookouts along the coast observed sails appearing on the horizon. They were quickly identified as British man-of-war vessels. By July 11, 1776, more than 130 ships were counted by scouts and observers and the British forces were estimated to be between 9,000 and 10,000 men. An invasion was anticipated daily by the Continental forces.

The local militia was called to arms by the firing of the cannon on Beacon Hill above the Springfields on First Mountain and the lighting of a tar barrel. General Washington ordered General William Livingston, who was in charge of the flying camp between Newark and Perth Amboy, to move all livestock from Staten Island before the British could land and to help residents who had not yet fled to move beyond the mountains. The flying camp was supposed to protect New Jersey from invasion. Unfortunately, it never had enough men to be truly effective. General Livingston of Elizabethtown, a lawyer, was elected the first governor of New Jersey in August 1776.

The British attacked Continental troops at Brooklyn Heights on Long Island and defeated them. The Continental Army pulled back to lower Manhattan Island, and the British followed. The Continental forces continued to pull back as far as White Plains—defeat followed defeat.

At White Plains, General Washington started to move south toward New Jersey. The British were in close pursuit, and forts fell. When Fort Washington on Manhattan Island on the Hudson River fell, General Washington ordered his men to leave Fort Lee in New Jersey, where they were camped. The Continental troops withdrew immediately, leaving food cooking over fires, cannon, cannon balls, bullets, blankets, and other supplies.

The army crossed over the Passaic River at Aquackanonk and finally arrived in Newark, where it camped for five days just north of Newark Town. Phillips, or Elwood Park on Summer Avenue and Elwood Place, was designated as the historic site by the City a century later. The camp apparently spilled over into present-day Branch Brook Park nearby. The bridge at Aquackanonk was burned after the last soldier crossed it.

General George Washington, followed by his Continental troops, rides through Newark in this depiction of his 1776 retreat.

The Old Powder Magazine stood on Heller Parkway at Woodside Avenue for more than 100 years near the area where both Continental and British troops camped in 1776.

The British army, delayed by the destroyed bridge, did not hurry. The remaining families in the town with their cattle, horses, chickens, some household goods, and, of course, family members fled beyond the mountains. General Washington continued into Newark Town, where he, according to local legend, walked through a cemetery, probably the Old Burying Ground near the Four Corners, with Thomas Paine, who reportedly composed *The Crisis* in Newark at Washington's request to encourage people to support the war effort.

The beginning of his essay, familiar to most schoolchildren, is "These are the times that try men's souls—the summer soldier and the sunshine patriot will, in this crisis, shrink from the service of his country, but he that stands now, deserves the love and thanks of man and woman. Tyranny, like hell, is not easily conquered."

One of the graves General Washington and Paine looked upon was that of Garrett Garrabrandt. The words on the stone read, "G.G. Overleiden." In local lore, the general asked the sexton what the inscription meant. The sexton answered, "Sir, that is the resting place of Garrett Garrabrandt. He worked hard clearing the land and planting his crops. He died overburdened by it all. Those were the times that tried men's bodies."

As General Washington and his troops left the town on November 28, the British troops were entering it. They occupied the same camping area as the Continental troops had used. They broke into the parsonage of Reverend Dr. Alexander Macwhorter and ripped his books, papers, and church records.

The British offered amnesty to those citizens who supported them. Tories marked their gateposts with the initial "R" to show that they were Royalists. The British paid little attention. The property damage was just as bad for the supporters of the Crown as for the rebels. The British entered some of the nicer homes and stole the furniture. In one supposed case, they removed a sick woman from her bed and took it. One man identified only as Nuttman met the British with joy, but the British troops ransacked his house and even took the shoes he was wearing off his feet. Later, Nuttman was jailed by the Continental forces at Morristown for his support of the British.

Newark and Elizabethtown were occupied for six weeks from November 29, 1776, to January 9, 1777, when the King's forces were ordered to Perth Amboy. Atrocities and skirmishes were frequent. The skirmishes were between as little as 2 or 3 men and 500 men, and several people died in these attacks. Others were terrorized and threatened with death. Fences and houses were torched, and cattle, horses, chickens, pigs, sheep, and other livestock were stolen.

Young Tories in the area joined the New Jersey Volunteers or General Cortland Skinner's Brigade of Loyalists on Staten Island, and several are reported to have led some of these raids to their former homes. A large attack occurred on September 10, 1777, when British forces marched through Elizabethtown to Newark as far as Second River (Belleville), stealing cattle, killing at least one person, and injuring several others. However, the British never seemed to trust

This large statue of General George Washington faces Broad Street and commemorates the route Washington took on his famous retreat in 1776.

the Loyalist troops or use them effectively. The Loyalists were never included in the British Army, and thus, they never truly formulated a spokesman to articulate the Loyalist's point of view.

General Washington had succeeded in making his retreat and made two daring and successful attacks on Trenton in the First and Second Battles and the Battle of Princeton and had gone into winter quarters at Morristown.

Some of Newark's Tories left town for the safety of New York City. One of these refugees was Justice David Ogden, who escaped to England, but returned to Long Island at war's end. Tory women were also suspect; the Continentals felt that they were spying for the King. They were given an opportunity to swear allegiance to the Continental Congress and continue to be peaceable residents or have their homes and land auctioned. In general, the new government felt that it would be best to send the women to their husbands. Some Tories returned in order to take the oaths of allegiance and to save their estates.

Women who supported the Continental cause and whose houses had been destroyed also posed a problem. If they had relatives beyond the mountains, they would move in with them for the duration, but many of them, with their children, followed their husbands into the camps. Some became useful as cooks, laundresses, or nurses, but many meant additional mouths to feed and proved problematic to move when the army wanted to attack or avoid a confrontation.

The Continental Army had its spies too. Two spies who operated in Newark were Stephen Ball, who was apprehended by the British and hanged, and Captain Caleb Bruen, who was able to discover how the British were planning to infiltrate the unhappy Pennsylvania line at Morristown, which planned to revolt because of poor conditions in the camp and lack of food and pay. Captain Bruen gained the trust of the British and was assigned to carry messages. By so doing, the revolt was avoided. He was, however, arrested by the British when he was unable to produce the proper letters and was then kept in the Old Sugar House Prison in New York City until the end of the war.

Small pox, the Bloody flux, and Camp Fever, in addition to filth and stench, were common to the wartime experience reported by the Tory prisoners in the jail at Morristown. A few prisoners were moved to better quarters at their own expense, and some efforts were made to clean the jail. Diseases were not limited to the Morristown jail or the Old Sugar House Prison in New York City; they spread through the camps on both sides, disabling and killing a large number of soldiers.

A raid on January 25, 1780, hit both Elizabethtown and Newark. The six-year-old Newark Academy, on what became Washington Park, was torched after 15 militiamen sleeping inside were taken prisoners. John Hedden Jr. was seized in his nightclothes from his home and made to walk barefoot across the meadows to New York City, where he was thrown into the Old Sugar House Prison. He was released some months later, but died September 27, 1780, at his home.

Newarkers participated in every battle during the eight years of war except for those around Boston. These included the last major battles in the North:

This tablet, dedicated in June 1916, marks the site of the Newark Academy, which was burned by the British on January 25, 1780.

Connecticut Farms on June 7, 1780, and the Springfields on June 23, 1780. In both instances, the British were attempting to reach Washington's ammunition and supply depot at Morristown, and they were stopped by the regular Continental army, augmented by the militiamen who were fighting to save their homes. The British were driven back to the Arthur Kill, where they had built a crude bridge of boats anchored together with logs on top as a roadway to Staten Island.

The war moved to the South where General Washington, with the aid of the French, defeated General Lord Charles Cornwallis in the battle at Yorktown in Virginia in October 1781. It took until November 25, 1783, Evacuation Day, before the British sailed out of New York City. During that time, Washington's troops watched the British from the West Windsor Cantonment at Vail's Gate, New York, until the Treaty of Paris was signed ending the war. Some skirmishes and raids for food continued, but there were no major conflicts. The Tories in turn sailed either to England, where 6,000 of them lived on small pensions and were unwelcomed by English society, or to Canada, where they were accepted but failed to receive any pensions. A few went to the West Indies and a few were able to resume their lives in their homes. The cost of loyalty was very high.

The American Revolution is the only war that the nation has fought on Newark soil. The War of 1812 and the Civil War (War Between the States) were to the

The Meeker Homestead was built in 1678 upon "Pot Pie Lane," renamed Chancellor Avenue for Chancellor Oliver Spencer Halsted, first chancellor of New Jersey.

south of Newark. The Indian Wars were to the west, while the Spanish-American, World Wars I and II, the Korean Conflict, the Vietnam War, and the Gulf War were hundreds of miles, even continents, away.

Throughout the Revolutionary War, the Town of Newark and Elizabethtown were subject to some 100 attacks. In addition to the armed personnel, thieves sometimes dressed in red coats and stole the townspeople's property. Some residents swung back and forth in their allegiances, depending upon which army was present. The Trinity Episcopal Church in Newark, like St. John's Episcopal Church in Elizabethtown, favored the Crown, but both had men who enrolled in the Continental Army and both structures served as hospitals during the war.

New immigrants tended to support the Crown. Loyalists also were people who wanted to preserve the status quo, were conservative, and feared change; they tended to be merchants in coastal trade, professionals such as physicians and lawyers, royal officials and office holders, and frontiersmen.

Three Revolutionary stories are particularly important and worthy of mention. Elihu Fish of New London, Connecticut, who had been captured while serving with the Connecticut forces, was released from the Old Sugar House Prison by the British, who ferried him to Elizabethport. His clothes were dirty and torn and his shoes, full of holes. His face was unshaven and he was sick and hungry.

Fish stopped at each house as he walked toward the Elizabethtown Presbyterian Church asking for food and money to return home. The people shunned him. He turned onto the Upper Road to Newark and continued walking. Finally, after what must have seemed like an eternity to him, he saw smoke from a chimney from the Meeker House up Pot Pie Lane. He turned and walked to the house. Three young girls were home. When they observed his condition, they invited him in and gave him food, warm water to wash, and finally a clean bed in which to sleep.

Fish was cared for by the sisters for a week. He questioned a brother about the family. After a while, he was able to travel. Years later, a well-dressed stranger appeared at the Meeker door. It was Elihu Fish with six sterling silver spoons, two for each sister, in appreciation of their care and kindness when he needed both.

In another story, Benjamin Coe, an older gentleman when the Revolution began, wanted to serve, but he was too infirmed. Instead, he sent his slave, Cudjo, who was among the 700 African-American soldiers at the Battle of Monmouth. At the war's end, when Cudjo arrived home safely, Coe gave Cudjo his freedom and an acre of land for a house on High Street, now Martin Luther King Jr. Boulevard. According to legend, Cudjo entered into a successful business life.

One of Newark's leading citizens during the Revolutionary War and for sometime afterward was Elisha Boudinot, brother of Elias Boudinot IV, president of the Continental Congress in 1782, when the Treaty of Paris was signed. His wedding to Catherine Smith, daughter of William Peartree Smith of Elizabethtown, in October 1778 was an outstanding social event, which General Washington and Marquis de Lafayette supposedly attended under guard.

The Benjamin Coe Homestead was located at the corner of Court and Washington Streets, near the site of the present Star-Ledger Building. The home was ransacked and burned by raiding British troops in 1776.

The young couple moved into a mansion on the site of the old Public Service Gas and Electric Company building on Park Place, built in 1916. The Smiths moved to Newark after their home in Elizabethtown was badly damaged in a raid. That house was the home of Royal Governor Jonathan Belcher and New Jersey State Governor Aaron Ogden. The Elizabethtown Historical Foundation currently owns the famous historic structure.

Lafayette wrote after the wedding that Catherine was married in her "old clothes." According to the story, Catherine was seeking a wedding dress from Europe apparently by "London trading," an illegal way of buying luxuries in the shadow of darkness from Staten Island. The dress failed to arrive and she wore one that she already owned. As for "London trading," it worked both ways. Sometimes farmers would provide fresh produce for the British army in the dead of night and perhaps receive tea in return. The Newark residents in turn would buy luxuries from England and Europe as Catherine had attempted to do. If caught, London traders were hanged.

President Elias Boudinot of the Continental Congress proclaimed a "Day of Thanksgiving" for the war's end on the second Thursday of December. This special day may be the first Federal Thanksgiving Day in the nation's history.

After the war, the people got to work, for so much had to be done. The sound of hammering was heard throughout the town as houses, barns, hen coops, mills, and other buildings burned or damaged during the war were rebuilt. Fences were installed; stores were restocked; flower and kitchen gardens were replanted; fields were plowed for new crops; schools and churches were rebuilt or repaired. Possessions hidden during the war were dug up, but in many instances, the family silver was never found. Flocks of sheep and chickens, herds of cows and other animals had to be replenished. Craftsmen had to make their products so that they could sell them. The people did not trust New Jersey's money so most transactions continued to be handled in barter.

Newarkers loved a parade then as they do now. The growing interest in business and industry, as well as patriotism, is reflected in the account of the July 4, 1788 celebration in Newark, published in the *New Jersey Journal* on July 9, 1788. The account records the event as follows:

> At sunrise the day was announced by a salute of 12 cannon, being the years of our independence, and the bells of different churches rang till 8 o'clock, when the independent corps, consisting of the Horse, Artillery, three companies of Frock Men, Grenadiers and infantry, commanded by Capt. [John Noble] Cumming, were paraded and reviewed; after the review they proceeded to the Presbyterian Church accompanied by the inhabitants of the place, where the Rev. Dr. Macwhorter delivered an elegant oration to a crowded audience. From the church, the procession being formed, they proceeded through the principal streets of the town, forming a line three quarters of a mile long; at one o'clock they reached the church green, when the artillery fired a salute of 10 cannon in honor

of the 10 Federal states. The Battalion fired the Feu-de Joy, which was returned by the inhabitants with three cheers.

The troops being divided into two parties after making the proper dispositions, a sham fight ensued, to the great entertainment and satisfaction of the spectators, then returned to a larger bower built on the occasion and partook of a cold collation. At 4 o'clock the clergy and other gentlemen of the town, with officers of different companies, partook of an elegant dinner provided by Mr. John Reading, when the following toasts were drank, accompanied by cannon, viz:

1. The United States
2. The 10 states that have adopted the New Constitution
3. The Government and State of New Jersey
4. General Washington, President of the late Convention
5. The officers and soldiers of the late American Army
6. The memory of the officers who fell in the late war
7. The officers and militia of Newark
8. The Farmers and Mechanics of Newark
9. May the Constitution last until days to come to an eternal pause, and sun and moon shall be no more.
10. The Day.

At night a painting of the head of George Washington was shown surrounded by the 10 states that had approved the Constitution. New York, Rhode Island and North Carolina had not yet approved it and were detached from the rest.

A procession followed, led by Nathaniel Camp and Caleb Wheeler. In this parade were representatives of some 25 trades, plus officials of the town, clergymen, lawyers, physicians, ship carpenters, merchants, and private gentlemen. Each trade was escorted by military officers. Many of the marchers were listed as journeymen and apprentices to that trade. Among them were cordwainers, joiners, quarrymen, stone cutters, masons, blacksmiths, scythe makers, coach and chairmakers, painters, wheelwrights, comb makers, silversmiths, clock and watch makers, tailors, hatters, saddlers and harness-makers, coopers, butchers, bakers, weavers, dyers, tobacconists, furnace men, millers, ship carpenters, constables, merchants, shopkeepers, private gentlemen, coroners, sailors, and a half troop of horse.

The whole was conducted with greatest decorum and regularity, not a dissatisfied countenance was seen, cheerfulness appeared in every face, and the day was spent in great hilarity, everyone viewing with each other who should be most agreeable.

In 1794, Prince Charles Maurice de Talleyrand Perigord, Bishop of Autun, arrived in Newark for a six-month visit and stayed with, of all people, the David Alling family, next to their furniture shop. He had been driven from France two

The original Lyons Farms School, a one-room schoolhouse, was burned during a British raid, and local farmers erected a new brownstone building in 1784.

years earlier and is said to have been an amateur chairmaker. During his stay, he visited the Lyons Farms School. Some say that he taught French while he was in New Jersey, as so many French did in that time period.

Elisha Boudinot was a judge in Newark and held several chairmanships during the war. He also was a leading fund-raiser for the rebuilding of the Newark Academy. His lovely home on Park Place was destroyed by fire in January 1797, and this conflagration caused Reverend Dr. Macwhorter and Reverend Uzal Ogden, rector of the Trinity Episcopal Church, to call a mass meeting of the citizens to form a volunteer fire department of two companies and one-hand pumper to battle the blaze.

Boudinot also was one of the leading citizens who entertained Marie Joseph Paul Yves Roch Gilbert du Motier, Marquis de Lafayette, a major general during the Revolutionary War, on his visit to Newark as the "Nation's Guest." Lafayette in his fourth trip to the United States from August 14, 1824, to September 6, 1825, toured all 24 states. Everywhere, he was met by the officials of the area, people with whom he had served in the war, bands, and large crowds. He is said to have seen his first steamboats when he was escorted across New York harbor from Staten Island to Manhattan Island after his arrival. The *Robert Fulton*, one of them, fired a 15-gun salute. He drove up Broadway in an open barouche under triumphant arches of flowers. Church bells rang. The reception in New York City continued for five days.

At a toll-gate on his way to Boston, the toll taker refused to accept the toll for his carriage. The keeper is quoted as saying, "You are the Nation's Guest." From that time on, he was not permitted to pay for his lodgings, meals, transportation, or other expenses. He was told, "All you want is supplied by a grateful people."

The Newark welcome began at Paulus Hook (Jersey City) at 9 a.m. on September 24, when he was met by a welcoming committee including Governor Isaac H. Williamson of Elizabethtown and members of the Second Division of the New Jersey Militia. He again rode in an open barouche drawn by four elegant bays. At Bergen, there was a salute by the artillery and a presentation of a cane made from a limb of an apple tree under which he and General Washington once refreshed themselves. The cane was mounted with gold and bore the inscription, "Shaded the hero and his friend, Washington in 1779, presented by the corporation of Bergen in 1824."

When he crossed the Bridge Street Bridge, opened in 1794, Lafayette was greeted by cheers of the throng assembled to welcome him. Adoring spectators lined the route to Judge Boudinot's rebuilt home, where lunch was served. Entering the parade ground, Lafayette and Governor Williamson passed between lines of 2,000 troops, the New Jersey Society of Cincinnati, the clergy, civil authorities, and citizens. A male chorus sang "the Approval." A band played and women and children threw flowers in his path. A chorus of 24 girls sang "the Welcome" as he approached a temple created for the occasion. The temple designed by Moses Ward was 40 feet in diameter and contained 13 arches, one for each of the original states. The dome symbolized the Western hemisphere. An

New Jersey Superior Court Judge Elisha Boudinot resided in this home on Park Place. Judge Boudinot also served as the president of the city's first bank, the Newark Banking and Insurance Building.

American eagle with a crown of laurels for peace on its head and an olive branch in one of its talons was on the top. Twelve beautiful bowers extended from each side of the temple to represent each of the states.

Attorney General Theodore Frelinghuysen gave the state's official welcome and told the story of Lafayette's participation in the Battles of Brandywine, Monmouth, and Yorktown. He also spoke of the years Lafayette spent as a prisoner in Austria during the French Revolution and his lifelong devotion to liberty for the common man.

Lafayette responded. Then, the troops passed in review before him under the command of Brigadier General Jonathan Dayton of Elizabethtown, the grand marshall. After the review, Lafayette greeted more than 5,000 citizens and it is reliably reported, in local lore, that his right hand was swollen because of the numerous handshakes.

Lafayette asked each of the people the name of his/her ancestor who had served with him during the Revolution. One young lady is said to have responded, "My grandfather and my father were loyal to the King!" Lafayette is said to have smiled at her and responded, "I'm glad to see that you have the courage to stand by the principles of your progenitors."

Parades marked the 50th anniversary of the Declaration of Independence on July 4, 1826. There were only a few of the veterans left and they rode in carriages along the parade route. Like the earlier parade in 1788, the paraders concluded the day by drinking many toasts to everybody and staggering home afterward, some to newly formed communities such as Orange, Bloomfield, and Livingston. Colonial Newark had ended. The Revolutionary War was coupled with Plymouth Rock as one of America's most important historical events.

Newark Town had grown by 1830 to a town of about 10,000. The town officials decided that it should be divided into four wards with two representatives from each ward. Three years later, on March 18, 1836, the town was rechartered as the City of Newark. It became the third city in the United States, behind Boston and New York. William Halsey, a lawyer, was elected the first mayor of Newark on April 11, 1836. He subsequently became judge of the Court of Common Pleas and served until his death on August 16, 1843, at age of 73.

By 1836, when Newark became a city, two wars against England had been won. The people of Newark no longer feared the loss of their soil to the Proprietors. They were looking westward. The Louisiana Purchase of 1803 had opened the West for settlement and trade. The construction of the Cumberland Road and the Erie Canal made westward travel easier. The Lewis and Clark expedition showed the possibilities of territory to be settled. A Newarker served as the first president in the early tentative government of the Republic of Texas and Dayton, Ohio, was named for Jonathan Dayton of Elizabeth, the youngest signer of the Constitution. Newarkers were eager for the future.

3. Made in Newark

Until well after the Revolutionary War, Newark's commercial life was limited to cottage industries conducted typically by a single craftsman assisted by a journeyman and one or two apprentices. They worked out of their homes, either living upstairs or behind their shops. These craftsmen were shoemakers, weavers, silversmiths, goldsmiths, clockmakers, cabinet makers, carriage makers, and chair makers, just to name a few. Both Elizabethtown and Newark Town had many tanners and were noted for the quality of their leather.

Samuel Whitehead of Elizabethtown is recorded as the first shoemaker in Newark in the seventeenth century. One account states that he failed to move to Newark because at that time, the shoemaker would stay in a household while he made the family's shoes and then move on to another residence to make shoes for that family. This account suggested that Whitehead, a family man, wished to stay with his own family and did not care to be a traveling man. The custom of a craftsman or woman moving in with a family was not unusual. As late as 1910, dressmakers would visit a family for a week to make the necessary dresses for the women and girls in the family.

Reverend Moses Combs made shoes during the day, and at night, he taught his apprentices free of charge. Combs built a school adjacent to his shoe manufacturing business on Market Street in 1790. His apprentices included both white and black youths. Combs also conducted a Sunday school class for the apprentices. Most of his students became successful businessmen, and many of them lived in Combs's home, as was the custom of the day. His school is considered by some historians to be the first vocational institution.

When Charles Basham, a teacher at Newark Academy, drew the shoemakers' map in 1806, he wrote that one third of Newark's inhabitants were engaged in shoemaking. In addition to shoes and boots, local businessmen also made leather work clothes and leather seats for chairs and coaches.

Reverend Moses Combs, one of Newark's successful shoemakers, established an evening vocational school for his apprentices in 1790.

One of the paintings reproduced in many books on Newark is that of David Alling's home and furniture shop. Alling was noted for making fancy side-chairs. It was his home that Charles Maurice de Talleyrand-Perigord, Prince de Benevent, visited during his exile from France. Talleyrand supposedly taught at the Lyons Farms School and participated in chairmaking at Alling's shop.

John Jeliff was known for making his almost ceiling-high clock cases for the popular grandfather clocks. There also were some 7 more cabinet makers, 6 more chair manufacturers, and some 29 coach makers in Newark.

There were several weavers of woolen goods in Newark, beginning with John Condict in 1695. At first, weavers were itinerant like the early shoemakers, and they used looms at the homes of the people they visited. Gradually, they established their own shops and their customers began coming to them. These early shops evolved into small factories of mass production for various materials and clothing. One of the first factories was opened by Thomas Owen in 1821 as the Washington Factory, which was destroyed by fire on January 4, 1822, with a loss of $10,000—a tremendous amount of money at that time.

Silversmiths, goldsmiths, and clock makers appeared in Newark in the late eighteenth century. Smith Burnet listed his skills in early advertisements in all three crafts. He must have been doing well because he advertised for a journeyman six months later, and nine months after that, he was seeking a clock maker. Benjamin Cleveland, who called himself both a silversmith and clock maker, advertised for two youths to assist him, and Cary Dunn sought work as both a goldsmith and silversmith.

The excellent quality of Newark jewelry made it one of the city's fastest growing industries. Epaphras Hinsdale organized a jewelry business on Broad Street near Lafayette Street after the Revolutionary War. John Taylor became his partner, and when Hinsdale died, Colonel Isaac Baldwin became Taylor's partner. Taylor and Baldwin's shop became the first regular jewelry factory in the city and had 100 workers. James Madison Durand served an apprenticeship at Taylor and Baldwin and then established his own company, Durand & Company, in 1828. There were 9 firms in 1845 and 50 firms in 1874. Aaron Carter was the first to use steam-powered machinery to make gold chains and watch cases. Many more firms were formed as new technologies were adopted. George Krementz, who invented the one-piece collar button to attach to a shirt, later specialized in costume jewelry, featuring pins, rings, bracelets, and neckwear. Krementz & Company closed in 1999. Tiffany and Company built a fortress-like structure in Newark, where it produced sterling silver items.

J. Wiss and Son opened in 1848 in Newark to manufacture shears and cutlery. In 1978, the company's shears and cutlery section was purchased by a Texas corporation and moved to North Carolina. Previously, the company had entered the jewelry business and opened a store on Broad Street, with an attractive

Employees of the Kolmar Jewelry Company in Newark pause so that the moment may be captured on film c. 1920. Louis Anselm is seated at left on the front row.

Seth Boyden was one of Newark's most celebrated inventors. His mind was always working to improve or invent something that would enhance life and work around him.

landmark pier clock in front of it. When the Short Hills Mall opened after World War II, the store followed the example of many of its trade and moved to the Morris Turnpike in Summit, where it continued to sell jewelry, fine China, and glassware for many years.

In 1860, Edward Balbach began separating gold and silver from other metals swept from the floor in the jewelry factories. His process of refining metals made him a rich man. The method also helped to produce pure lead necessary for the emerging paint industry and helped in the making of platinum by Daniel W. Baker and Charles Engelhard, who opened refineries in 1875.

Newark became the center of heavy industry when Seth Boyden arrived in 1815. Boyden established a shop at his home on Bridge Street, near the bridge, the first one to cross the Passaic River at Newark. Boyden was the consummate problem solver, and after he had solved a particular dilemma, he would start a company to market his solution, sell the company, and then go onto another problem.

Before coming to Newark, Boyden had developed a method for splitting leather so that more leather was produced from a single piece. In Newark, he observed the peaked caps of some officers, and he invented patent leather that could be used for shoes, bags, or the caps. He developed a drying oven to dry the hats or shoes faster. He created a silver-plating process for his harnesses so that the harnesses would not rust. Then, Boyden began finding ways to make malleable iron—iron that could be bent. He worked for six years with various pig irons after he closed his doors for the night on his patent leather business until he found a way to make a cheap workable metal for harness buckles.

Then, another problem attracted his attention. The Morris and Essex Railroad was being constructed and it needed engines to carry the cars over the mountains.

He built two steam engines: the *Essex* and the *Orange*. He put the connecting rods on the outside of the driving wheel instead of on the axle inside the wheel. This leverage was more direct and it was successful. The third and last engine he made was transported to Cuba.

He became interested in daguerreotype photographs, made a camera, and began experimenting. Samuel Morse joined him in cutting the exposure time. Morse also received some help from Boyden on the electric telegraph. Boyden then applied to the United States Patent Office for a patent on a stationary steam engine for the Newark Lime and Cement Company with a cut-off valve. He did not receive the patent because he had failed to build a model of the proposed improvement.

New Jersey possessed deposits of copper, iron, and zinc when it was settled. The copper and iron had run out or became too expensive to mine, but the zinc was there if it could be smelted cheaply. Again, Boyden solved the problem.

During his long career, he had few failures, but he sold his companies as soon as the discovery was prepared for the marketing. Although he could have had millions from his successful solutions and innovative ideas, he was always poor. When questioned, he was said to have answered that the inventions belonged to the world, not to him.

Sacks-Barlow Foundry on Wilson Avenue claimed descent from Boyden's achievements. William Watts of Watts Campbell Company, a machine shop that is still in business, was an apprentice of Boyden until he left to start his own company.

The Watts Campbell Company, started in 1851, continues to make machinery.

Karl Gerhardt produced this statue in Washington Park to honor the life and industrial legacy of Seth Boyden.

After a futile trip to California in search for gold with the other "49ers," Boyden and his son returned home. The family moved to Hilton, now a section of Maplewood, where Boyden became interested in growing strawberries. He managed to grow the largest ones ever produced.

On one occasion, Boyden was approached by a contemporary who was enamored of a young woman and wanted to appear younger than he was, so he asked Boyden to develop a dye for his hair. Boyden experimented, and when he believed he had found the perfect dye, he poured it on the man's head. It was black and beautiful. Unfortunately, by the next day, it had turned purple.

Boyden is credited by historian Charles F. Cummings for making Newark an industrial city. A bust of Boyden was presented at Newark's first industrial exposition on August 29, 1872. A statue of him by Karl Gerhardt was dedicated in Washington Park on May 14, 1890. It is the only statue in the city of a man in working clothes; he is wearing his leather apron.

The diversification of manufacturing and the improvement of transportation in the early part of the nineteenth century made the town officials realize that the town had outgrown the old form of government, the town meeting. The area was flourishing and expanding. A referendum was conducted to determine if Newark should become a city. It passed, and the City of Newark was incorporated in 1836 as the third city in the nation.

James Jay Mapes, an outstanding scientist and foremost agriculturist of his day, introduced the use of chemical fertilizers and obtained a patent for use of phosphates on his experimental farm on the Upper Road to Elizabethtown. He invented a plow that lifted sub-soil, and he studied and distributed seeds for sweet corn. The results of his efforts were reported in a magazine he edited, the *Working Farmer*, from 1849 to 1854.

Agrarian Newark was changing. While Mapes was worrying about better production on the farms, the number of foundries and chemical plants was increasing, and although there was an increase in the number of craftsmen, mass production and assembly lines were just around the corner in Newark's industrial future.

In addition to the cider mills popular in seventeenth and eighteenth centuries, the nineteenth century witnessed the growth of breweries. General John N. Cumming had started a brewery at High and Orange Streets about 1799. Its name changed to Morton's in 1840, when it was purchased by Peter Ballantine, a Scot who built a new plant near the Passaic River on Rector Street. Soon, he had competition from the Germans who were moving into the area. The first German competitor was John N. Schalk, who arrived in 1849 and established a brewery at Napoleon Street and Hamburg Place. His sons later moved the brewery to Bowery and Ferry Streets.

Morton's Brewery on High Street was an outgrowth of the first brewery opened by John N. Cumming in the early part of the nineteenth century.

Wearing hats and vests under their coats, employees of the Peter Ballantine & Company pose for this group photo.

The Ballantine brewery expanded and moved Down Neck next to the Morris Canal and became the largest brewery in the nation. It survived the Prohibition era and in the 1940s and 1950s was known for hiring college students during the summertime. It closed in 1969. Parts of the landmark building have been demolished, while the rest is used by commercial enterprises.

Gottfried Krueger and Christian Feigenspan both started as apprentices with Laible and Adam. They later opened their own breweries and were both very successful. In all of Newark, there were some 26 breweries in 1879 to serve the German community of some 35,000 persons. Joseph Hensler, another brewer, built both his house and brewery close to Hensler Street, which was named for him. At that time, as with the cottage industries earlier, many factory owners built their factories adjacent to their homes, for there was no zoning.

Anheuser-Busch Company, which moved to Routes 1 and 9, opposite the Newark International Airport after World War II, is the only brewery left in Newark. It sought to buy the land in 1946, and the facility has expanded since its initial construction.

The Civil War destroyed the Southern markets of Newark's industries, which began manufacturing articles for the Federal army. Boots, saddles, uniforms, wagons, and other equipment were made to meet the needs of the servicemen.

The Anheuser-Busch Company Brewery on Routes 1 and 9 was built after World War II and is the only brewery left in the city of Newark.

Franklin Murphy, a veteran of the Civil War and state governor from 1902 to 1905, organized the successful Murphy Varnish Company in 1891.

Franklin Murphy, state governor from 1902 to 1905, began a successful varnish-manufacturing factory after the Civil War. He is considered to be the "Father of the Essex County Parks System." He urged the building of the Passaic Valley Trunk sewer in 1912, sought to end pollution of the Passaic River, and fought to improve tenement housing, abolish child labor, and strengthen public schools. He was a leader in the investment of state funds so that they would earn interest, and he also set business hours for the state offices.

Paint manufacturers including Benjamin Moore, Sherwin Williams, Beckwirth-Chandler, Cook and Dunn, Flood and Conklin, Maas and Waldstein, Security Paint and Varnish, Vita-Var, Duralock Chemical Corporation, and Tribault and Walker also helped make Newark the paint and varnish center of the nation.

Thomas Alva Edison, born in Milan, Ohio, is one of the most influential inventors of modern time. Having spent only a few months in formal educational institutions, Edison was primarily home schooled by his mother. While living in Port Huron, Michigan, Edison began working at an early age for the Grand Trunk Railroad selling newspapers and candy and experimenting with publishing a newspaper. During Edison's time with the railroad, a station official taught him to operate the telegraph. Later, in his early twenties, Edison came to the East Coast to work as a telegrapher in Boston in 1868 and then moved to New York City the following year. He came to Newark in the winter of 1870, when he was 23 years old, to go into business for himself inventing things.

Edison was always busy questioning how something might be done better. He also invented an electric vote recorder, which Congress refused. He resided with Franklin Pope in Elizabeth while working in New York. Pope and Edison established a laboratory, and they worked on some electrical devices for Western Union, who purchased the lab. Edison was given some money for his work, and it was with this money that he was able to rent space at 4-6 Ward Street, Newark, for his own business. He continued to experiment and soon held some 34 patents; among them were improvements on the typewriter, an initial telephone, and an early model of the phonograph.

In 1876, Edison opened a research laboratory at Menlo Park. He received 300 patents in the seven years he was in Menlo Park. One of these was his first phonograph record on which even today one may hear his voice recite "Mary had a little lamb" at his last laboratory in West Orange, now a historic site.

Edison wanted to light the villages, and he worked on the electric light bulb. By 1879, he had perfected the first practical incandescent lamp at Menlo Park, which burned for 40 hours. Then, he wanted to apply this lamp to a village setting and he needed to create a power source—a generating plant. A year later, he lighted 35

Thomas A. Edison held more than 1,000 patents for items he or his employees had invented. His first laboratory was located on Mechanic Street, now Edison Place.

dwellings in what became Roselle and Charlie Stone's grocery store in the future Roselle Park. A chandelier, which is still in use today, was placed in the First Presbyterian Church in the Roselle section.

Later, Edison lighted the Pearl Street area of New York City and several other cities. His first wife, Mary Stillwell, a factory girl, died, and he married Mina Miller, a rich woman. He built houses in Fort Myers, Florida, and Llewellyn Park in West Orange. After moving his laboratory to West Orange in 1887, he perfected the motion picture camera and shot the first motion pictures made in New Jersey. In all, Edison held some 1,093 patents. He died on October 21, 1931. All the children in Newark's public schools were taken to their respective auditoriums for a moment of silence.

The leaders of Newark, proud of the city's industries, decided they would sponsor an industrial exhibition showing only Newark-made products. The exhibit was conducted at a skating rink on Washington Street and featured hundreds of products made in Newark's factories and by Newark craftsmen. The exhibit ran from August 20 to October 22, 1872. There were some 875 persons and firms participating. President U.S. Grant and Horace Greeley, editor of the *New York Tribune*, attended. Some 1,000 different articles were shown, and sales of these were excellent and the exhibit was pronounced a success.

Exhibits were conducted in 1873, 1874, and 1875, but discontinued in 1876, because of the nation's Centennial Exhibit in Philadelphia and the anticipated costs of entering both. The exposition was repeated in 1916, when Newark observed its 250th anniversary of the settlement in a year-long celebration.

The post–Civil War years witnessed the growth of industry in Newark. George A. Clark, another Scottish gentleman, founded the Clark Thread Company in Newark in 1864. He built a large factory beside the Passaic River in 1866 to manufacture thread. The company used the initials O.N.T. meaning "Our New Thread." Business was so good that Clark built factories across the river in Harrison and East Newark. The Newark factory, long vacant, was razed in 1999.

John Wesley Hyatt formed the Celluloid Company in 1868 on Ferry Street after experimenting with cellulose nitrate and acetate. The company manufactured raw materials and made plastic collars, cuffs, pipe bits, beer scrapers, organ stop keys, bracelets, and combs. Later, it developed sheets of wrapping material. In 1928, the company was purchased by the Celanese Corporation of America. Celluloid manufacturing ceased in 1949, and the plant was sold to a German firm, American Hoechst, in the 1980s and moved to Somerville as Hoechst Celanese Corporation.

George Mennen, a native of Germany, opened a drugstore in Newark in 1878. Soon he was making and selling products to treat corns and talcum powder for infants to prevent diaper rash. Mennen continued to make and sell such products until he gave up the drugstore to devote his full time to the manufacture of toiletries for men with his son, William.

Reverend Hannibal Goodwin, rector of the House of Prayer at 407 Broad Street at State Street, invented flexible film in his attic laboratory in 1887. The

Edward Weston, founder of Weston Electrical Instrument Company, produced streetlights for Newark, meters, and numerous other electrical improvements.

film became the basis of both the motion picture and still picture industry. Celluloid Company attempted to enter the film market but lost in a court fight with the Eastman Kodak Company in a dispute over the patent. Reverend Goodwin's widow received a settlement years after his death.

Edward Weston started an electrical machinery plant in a former synagogue on Washington Street in 1877. Later, he built a factory on Frelinghuysen Avenue at Haynes Avenue for a huge plant to make electrical instruments, including light meters for cameras. The factory produced underground cables, batteries and fuses, generators and motors, and streetlights.

The city's industry turned again to war production during the Spanish-American War and World War I. The war with Spain began in April 1898, and President William McKinley's call for volunteers was answered by Newark's youth. They marched by a cheering crowd to trains at the Central Railroad of New Jersey Station on Broad Street near Market Street and were taken to Sea Girt, the state's training ground. Transferred to Camp Alger, Virginia, near Washington, the regiment was honorably discharged in September after the Spanish forces had surrendered at Santiago, Cuba.

Louis Aronson moved to Newark in 1895 to establish the Art Metal Works, where he invented a time fuse for airplane bombs and a wind-proof match in

Young women in an unidentified factory take a moment from their work to perform some exercises c. 1900.

World War I. He also developed fireless fireworks and received a Victory medal in World War I for the Ronson cigarette lighter. He was awarded a prize by the Belgian government for inventing a match without phosphorous.

World Wars I and II caused old factories to retool for manufacture of items for the wars and new factories to be organized and to work 24 hours daily. The Submarine Boat Company began building ships for the war effort at Port Newark, and 52 ships were constructed by January 1920.

There were shortages of both skilled and unskilled workers for these various factory jobs. African Americans came north from Georgia, Alabama, and the Carolinas to fill some of these jobs and stayed after the wars ended. While they were wanted in the factories to do the heavy work, they were not wanted by the local community in its neighborhoods and so they were confined to the oldest houses in the center city, where several families might have to share the same facilities. These black families and newcomers were charged high rents for sub-standard shacks and basement apartments.

Women began doing non-traditional work in the shipyard in World War I for the first time, long before Rosie the Riveter, America's symbol for the female worker. Again, during World War II, the factories relied heavily on a female workforce.

Unfortunately, the war to end all wars did not. Twenty years later, in response to the war in Europe, America began to gear up for battle again. As early as 1940, the government was signing contracts with Newark clothing factories for overcoats, jackets, and ties for the army, for military insignia for the uniforms, aircraft instruments, zippers, tents, military field telephones, radio parts, fuses, and many other items. The federal government purchased the old Submarine Boat Company site for the Federal Shipbuilding Company, which built destroyers, destroyer escorts, and troop landing ships. In order to meet the contract requirements, firms such as Westinghouse and Weston extended their hours, working two or three shifts instead of one.

At one time, Newark had 90 firms engaged in making electrical goods and machinery. Largest of these were General Electric Company, which moved in 1953, and the Westinghouse Electric Company. International Telephone and Telegraph Company has facilities in at least nine municipalities besides Newark. Formed in 1885, American Telephone and Telegraph (AT&T) was the world's largest firm in the communications business until the federal court mandated its break-up in the 1980s. Since that decision, AT&T and the "seven baby bells" have continued to splinter or to rejoin each other, while other companies have formed to compete with them. New Jersey Bell Telephone Company has become Verizon through mergers and still has a large office in Newark.

Thomas N. McCarter Jr. formed Public Service Electric and Gas Company (PSE&G) in 1903 by buying numerous small gas and electric companies and formed Public Service Coordinated Transport by purchasing tiny bus and trolley lines and combining them into long lines. There were 521 companies involved in these transactions.

The Public Service Electric and Gas Company and Public Service Transport erected this building opposite Military Park in 1916.

An employee watches the assembly line of milk bottles at the Alderney Dairy in Newark.

The men who read and serviced the gas meters for the PSE&G rode bicycles from place to place at first. Sometimes, the rides would be from Summit to Paterson or Montclair or Summit to Newark, Harrison, and Morristown. The bicycles were replaced by automobiles in the mid-twenties. In interviews in *The Energy People: A History of PSE&G* by James and Richard Conniff, some of the former employees said they would ride a train with their bicycles when possible and then ride to the designated site.

Although the Depression caused many factories to close in Newark, other companies soon took their places. Despite the move out of the city or out of state by many of the businesses, there are still more than 150 large factories, more than 200 warehouses, and an assortment of others, such as one leather company, one large kosher food company, paint and pigment companies, several chemical companies, a doll company, jewelry and corrugated box manufacturers, cabinet makers, plastic and steel products, coat and knitwear manufacturers, door manufacturers, and even a milk company. At this time, Continental Airlines is the city's largest employer.

The diverse manufacturers in Newark created a need for the availability of cash and insurance in case of disaster. Newark's first bank was the Newark Banking and Insurance Company in 1804. New Jersey chartered state banks in 1812, including the Newark State Bank. Others were opened in Elizabethtown, Camden, Trenton, New Brunswick, and Morristown. Later, these banks became

National Banks. The First National State Bank of New Jersey merged in 1983 with Fidelity Union Bancorp to become First Fidelity Bank. First Fidelity Bank has merged with First Union National Bank.

At one time, banks were limited to small territories, usually only the counties in which they were located. Since 1990, when the laws were changed, banks have crossed state lines. The Summit Bancorp is the largest commercial bank solely located in New Jersey. Others that serve the state are based in other areas. United Jersey Bank has merged with the Summit Bank. The PNC Bank has absorbed the Midlantic Bank, while Chemical Bank joined Chase Manhattan. NatWest has become part of Fleet Bank.

Savings banks had become popular for the general public, as the immigrants began depositing some of their assets for a rainy day, to send money home to a family member, or to pay the passage for those who hoped to join them in the new world. Building and Loans were formed to help finance the many new homes that immigrants were purchasing in the Ironbound and other sections of the city. Of note, there was the Susan B. Anthony Savings & Loan, formed by women, truly unusual for its time. Another form of banking was the federal credit union, organizations of employees of a business, industry, organization, or church that pooled their savings to make loans to themselves at low rates of interest.

The Mutual Benefit Life Insurance Company was founded in 1845. Several other insurance companies followed it briefly. They included the Newark Mutual Fire Insurance Company, Fire Merchants Insurance Company, the New Jersey Plate Glass Insurance Company, and the Germania Insurance Company.

First Fidelity Bank appears in this bird's-eye view of downtown Newark taken in 1986.

This early-twentieth-century scene of Broad Street shows the imposing Prudential Building.

John Dryden started the Prudential Insurance Company in the mid-1870s, and it was one of the first insurers and became one of the largest. In addition to handling property, casualty, and health insurance, it has acquired Bache Securities Inc. and entered the securities market, administers the federal Medicare program in New Jersey and some other states, and is involved in real estate investments. Prudential has expanded its market across the nation, but its headquarters continue to be located in Newark, where it serves as a major contributor to Newark's arts and culture.

The Firemen's Insurance Company began in 1810. In 1868, the company built an ornate Victorian structure at the corner of Broad and Market Streets, with a hand-carved fireman on the tower. Unfortunately, it was demolished and a skyscraper was built near the present site of the New Jersey PAC about 1910. With 16 stories, this old skyscraper, considered to be the city's first, has been restored. Other insurers in the city include Allstate, Aetna, Met Life, Liberty Mutual Group, Mutual of Omaha, and State Farm. Horizon Blue Shield and Blue Cross has stayed in Newark to continue to serve its customers

Newark was changing. Buildings were stretching upward. The ornate, gray Prudential Building on Broad Street went up in 1892 with its towers, gargoyles, and medieval decorations. A drinking fountain for the public was available at the corner of the building. A new structure for the United States Post Office was erected in 1890 on Broad Street at Academy Street, adjacent to the Morris Canal to replace Library Hall, where the mail had been handled. This edifice stood until the Federal Building, with the post office, was erected behind Grace Episcopal Church in the 1930s. The 12-story Kinney Building was erected across the street from the site of the old Firemen's Insurance Company Building at the Four Corners in 1912. The National State Bank erected a slim 10-story building next to the First Presbyterian Church, whose steeple was at the same level. The New Jersey Bell Telephone Company building at 540 Broad Street, the Military Park Building, and the Robert Treat Hotel went up in the 1920s, and the Lefcourt building and the National Newark and Essex Building were completed in the early 1930s. The Prudential erected a new office building on Washington Street that was used by the Office of Dependency Benefits throughout World War II.

Until World War I, most of the business leaders resided in Newark either along High Street or in Forest Hill. A few had ventured onto Clinton Hill and along Elizabeth Avenue in the Weequahic section, where several spacious homes were being erected after 1910. The move to Maplewood and Millburn (Short Hills), East Orange and South Orange, Summit and Westfield began in the 1920s.

Dr. Paul Stellhorn of the Newark Public Library places Newark's decline in the mid-1920s. Newarkers enjoyed the Roaring Twenties and many even found excitement in the Depression thirties. During World War II, many of the citizens appeared to work together for one single purpose: to win the war. In Lauder's, a jewelry firm making parts for airplanes, a special night shift employed Portuguese Mary, German Mary, Irish Mary, three teachers, a widow, and her sister. The

A delivery truck from the Hudson Super Cord Tires Company, one of Newark's various businesses, is pictured here on Washington Street.

foreman was a Jewish high school football coach waiting to join the armed forces, and they all got along.

When the war ended, there were changes. The war had introduced the world to the young people who served and they wanted to live in it, not near their parents. These ex-GIs sought cheaper housing, so they went outside the city, where they purchased small houses with plenty of land for the growth of their families. Institutions such as churches and clubs suffered losses of membership. Many never recovered. If they did, they were not the same.

Newark's industry attracted more and diverse industrialists to the city. It also attracted workers seeking better salaries. Noted for its variety of products, the economy of the city has never depended upon a single industry. Like Reverend Combs, the industrialist and educators have been interested in training and retraining workers to fill these varied jobs and to meet the demands of the twenty-first century as they did those of the nineteenth and twentieth centuries. Industries are constantly changing. Numerous new buildings are being constructed or older ones restored in the South Ward for these new businesses.

Located on Frelinghuysen Avenue, Weston Electrical Instrument Company offered shop mathematics class at their work.

4. Transportation Hub

Until the swamps between Newark and Jersey City were conquered, the best and fastest way to New York City was by boat: down the Passaic River to Newark Bay, across the bay to the Kill Van Kull between Bayonne and Staten Island, and into New York Harbor probably to the Battery. The distance was perhaps 12 miles, but the time depended upon the wind and the weather.

The Provincial legislature authorized the installation of the Newark Plank Road from Newark to Paulus Hook (Jersey City) in 1765 and the operation of ferries across the Passaic and Hackensack Rivers. Huge rough boards were placed across the roads in hopes that the wagon wheels would pass over them without being mired in the mud. Nothing held the boards in place and they could shift.

Matthias Ward of the Ward Stage Wagon was given the contract to carry passengers on daily round trips to Paulus Hook. The wagons were heavy. Benches were provided as seats for the passengers. It took four to six horses to pull a single wagon. The passengers were protected from the weather only by a canvass or cloth roof. Eventually, the wagons were improved. The body was raised and the width reduced. Regular seats and finally springs were installed. When springs were invented, the wagon bodies were suspended on the springs, making it a much more comfortable ride.

Later, stagecoaches were developed, and these too provided a more comfortable ride when springs were installed. The stagecoaches could only carry five passengers and baggage. Their big advantage was that they were enclosed carriages with roofs. Thomas Brown held a franchise to operate ferries for the carriages across the Passaic and Hackensack Rivers.

Despite these improvements, the passengers, usually only men, frequently had to dismount and help push the wagons or carriages out of the mud. Sometimes, they were requested to walk up hills because the combined load of men and baggage was too heavy or the road was too slippery for the horses. Snow-covered

Horses and wagons, electric trolley cars, motor cars, and trucks vie for space on this Newark street in 1918.

roads were favored because then runners could be placed on the vehicle, which would glide over the road. The roads were rutted much of the year.

The Newark Plank Road followed the route of the present Ferry Street. The rough logs were replaced by smooth planks in 1849, giving the road its name. Tolls were charged. Ferry Street now is the main business district in the Ironbound section of Newark. A road linked the Newark Plank Road with the Old York Road in Elizabethtown.

The state assembly also approved a road between Elizabethtown Point and the Raritan River. This road became Route 27, which went along Frelinghuysen Avenue in Newark. It was called the old Lincoln Highway before World War I. Except for buildings along it, the road between Elizabeth and Rahway is little changed. However, road construction has altered the roadway between Rahway and Highland Park, which crossed the Raritan River into New Brunswick and continued to Trenton and Philadelphia. Eventually, the roadway went across the country to become the first highway on which the new automobiles traveled to the West Coast.

The Crane & Davenport Wagon Line between Philadelphia, Newark, and New York City began operation about 1769. The wagon stopped at Elizabethtown, Bound Brook, North Branch of the Raritan River to Corriell's Ferry at Lambertville on the Delaware River, York in Pennsylvania, and Philadelphia. The route became known as the Old York Road. The wagons seldom traveled more than 12 miles a day, and the passengers would have to stay overnight at an inn. The accommodations were usually overcrowded with several men sharing the same bed. When women traveled, they were entertained in separate dining rooms from the men.

The tap rooms of these inns along the roads became the gathering places for both travelers and residents and the main source of news for the communities around them. Mail and newspapers were distributed at the inns.

People loved speed even before race cars. One of the early speed achievements was the establishment of Skillman "Flying Machine" Line in 1771. The trip from Newark to Bristol, Pennsylvania, took only a day and a half with stops at Elizabethtown, Woodbridge, New Brunswick, Princeton, and Trenton. The next year, the Philadelphia Coach Line began. Now U.S. Route 1, the road was first called the King's Highway because it was built to carry the King's troops. Several roads were so designated, which makes it difficult for today's map readers to trace the original paths. Route 1, however, is the first to go from Calais, Maine, to Key West, Florida, along the Atlantic coast. The newer Route 95 follows basically the same route. In Newark, the two roads are only a few feet apart.

The turnpike age dawned after 1800. New roads stretched out of Newark like a fan. The Morris Turnpike spur from Springfield to Newark was included in construction of the Morris Turnpike from Morristown to Elizabethtown in 1806.

This 1934 Chevrolet Roadster, like many of the early automobiles, offered the open road to all travelers. This particular model contained a rumble seat, providing additional space for two passengers, but exposing them to the elements.

The Mount Pleasant Turnpike Company created another large road, and this route went along Market Street to the old Crane Road to the main highway in Orange, where it branched off onto Mount Pleasant Avenue to Livingston enroute to Morristown. Other turnpikes also were built during this period to Orange up Orange Street and to Bloomfield up Bloomfield Avenue.

Canal fever swept the nation after the successful Erie Canal was opened and literally carried hordes of people West. New Jerseyans began to consider canals also, and two were built: the Delaware Raritan Canal from the Delaware River at Trenton to the Raritan River at New Brunswick and the Morris Canal from Phillipsburg to Jersey City. Like the Morris Turnpike, the Morris Canal was supposed to be cut originally from Morristown to Elizabethtown, a much easier route than by way of Paterson. Both Paterson and Newark wanted to be included on the canal's path. Political forces prevailed and the engineering marvel went by way of Paterson to Newark. The canal was completed in 1831 to Phillipsburg. It carried coal from the Pennsylvania mines to Newark, changing the way people heated their houses and replacing waterpower by steam in factories. It also carried produce from the farms and manufactured goods from the cities to the farms. The canal was built by private investors known as the Morris Canal and Banking Company. The laborers, more than 1,100 of them, were mostly Irish Roman Catholic men who came to this nation to make their fortunes. They built a shantytown Down Neck. When not busy with a pick and shovel digging the 3-foot, later the 4-foot, path from river to sea, they were noisy, drunk, and boisterous. The townspeople viewed them with distaste and did their best to avoid them, while at the same time being awed by the results of their work.

The canal, designed by George P. MacCulloch, was unique because it had to climb to Lake Hopatcong, a manmade lake from two ponds, 913 feet above sea

The Lock 17 was one of two locks in Newark on the 106-mile-long Morris Canal. The Morris Canal, chartered in 1824 and opened in 1832, brought boats loaded with coal, iron, wood, and vegetables.

level and down again. In order to accomplish this feat, the canal had 34 locks and 23 inclined planes to raise and lower the barges. Unlike the Erie Canal, the Morris Canal went both over and under bridges and railroads. It was 32 feet wide at the top of the canal, 10 feet wide at the bottom, and 4 feet deep. When completed to Jersey City, the canal was 106.80 miles long.

The canal entered Newark by crossing Second River and the Orange Branch line of the Erie, Lackawanna and Western Railroad at Lock 15 at Howe Street, Bloomfield. It traveled at ground level through the Silver Lake section of Newark along the future western border of Branch Brook Park and went under Bloomfield and Park Avenues. At Searing and Lock Streets in Newark, Lock 16B lowered the barges to the plane passing High Street (Martin Luther King Boulevard) to Plane Street, now University Avenue. The canal went underground at Broad Street between the United States Post Office and L.S. Plaut Department Store, under the City Central Market, built in 1848, to 17E, toward the site of the present Pennsylvania Station and returned to ground level. It went under the Jackson Street bridge and back to ground level once more to the city docks at 18E on Passaic River, to Canal Street at 19E, then 1,000 feet to Lock 20E at the foot of today's Raymond Boulevard.

The barges on the canal offered a pleasant outing for the people, who would take short rides on them. The canal was used also by locals for swimming during warm weather. The more daring boys went "stemming." They would put their feet against the prow of the barge and be pushed along on their backs through the water. The towpaths were used as bridle and bicycle trails. In winter, when the canal froze, it was used for ice skating.

The families of the barge captains usually accompanied them on their trips. In one case, a captain's wife, with her two children, joined her husband for her first ride. When the cable broke at an incline plane, the barge careened down the plane, jumped over the canal bank, and crashed on dry land. The captain's wife observed, "It was a mighty fast trip, but I thought that was the way the thing worked!"

The canal needed a good supply of water from Lake Hopatcong to operate and in the winter the surface froze. While it was pleasant for the skaters, it was bad for people who wanted to move the coal and other cargo. Railroad trains that could run all year and travelled faster began replacing the canal, making it eventually useless. Finally, in 1924, the canal was abandoned and became Raymond Boulevard, named for the Mayor Thomas L. Raymond. The canal bed below the boulevard became the Newark City subway.

Lake Hopatcong, the largest lake in New Jersey, was a summer vacation spot. Many of the summer cabins have been converted into permanent homes with the construction of super highways leading to New Jersey's lake district. There are an estimated 500 lakes in the area. Like Lake Hopatcong, many of them were made by damming streams.

Newark was served by several railroads by the nineteenth century. The New Jersey Railroad and Transportation Company completed the first track between Jersey City and Newark by 1834. It later became the Pennsylvania Railroad, which

The Delaware, Lackawanna, and Western Railroad Station, seen here c. 1900, is now operated by the New Jersey Transit.

leased the Camden & Amboy Railroad, the state's first railroad. A tunnel to New York City was opened in 1911.

The Elizabethtown and Somerville Railroad, later the Central Railroad of New Jersey, reached Plainfield by 1839 and Phillipsburg by 1852. A spur from Elizabethport served the Broad Street Station in Newark, and it was known for its summer excursion trains to the New Jersey shore.

The Morris and Essex, later the Delaware, Lackawanna and Western Railroad (DLW), reached Morristown in 1838, Dover in 1848, and Phillipsburg in 1865. Patrons of the DLW used to say the letters stood for "Delay, Linger, and Wait." The Erie Railroad later became part of this company.

The Lehigh Valley Railroad was founded in 1846 and ran between Mauch Chunk, Pennsylvania, and Easton, Pennsylvania. The railroad gradually pushed its way across New Jersey toward tidewater, until it was stalled at South Plainfield and Metuchen. In 1872, it leased the Morris Canal and installed tracks close to it, competing with the Morris and Essex Railroad. Until it could complete its own route, the Lehigh used the tracks of the Pennsylvania and New Jersey Central Railroad to reach New York City.

The Lehigh Valley Railroad acquired the property of the bankrupt New Jersey West Line Railroad Company, and the first train ran over them in 1891 from Newark to Jersey City. The West Line Railroad, chartered in 1870, was to have traveled from Pennsylvania to tidewater at Jersey City via Bernardsville, Summit, Springfield, Union, Lyons Farms, to Newark through what became Weequahic Park. The DLW later acquired its tracks west of Summit.

Newarkers, who had freed all their slaves by 1860, did have a large trade with the many slaveholding Southern states, so many locals weren't interested in war, and many even opposed the election of Abraham Lincoln. However, when President-elect Lincoln visited Newark enroute to Washington to assume office, he was welcomed by an enthusiastic throng of people. Mayor Moses Bigelow greeted him at the Morris and Essex Station on North Broad Street, and he was taken along Broad Street in an open carriage to the Chestnut Street Station for another train.

The bridging of the rivers, the improvement of the road to Paulus Hook (Jersey City), the extension of the Morris Turnpike from Springfield to Newark, the formation of other turnpikes, the growth of the railroads, and the port all helped to make Newark instead of Elizabethport the center of transportation in New Jersey and caused the city to grow and to become the largest city in the state.

The Civil War proved to be a railroad war. Troops and equipment were moved by rails, and since many of the soldiers from Newark were in Virginia or Pennsylvania, it was possible for them to take a train home for the weekend and return to the battlefield by Monday morning. The closeness to rapid transportation also allowed several who were wounded to return to Newark for nursing at home or in the new Marcus Ward Hospital.

A passenger train is seen here passing the second Pennsylvania Station on elevated tracks. The railroad industry would transform the city and the nation.

Major General Philip Kearny, known as the "One-Armed Devil," was a magnificent Union leader during the Civil War.

Marcus Ward had arranged for a building on Centre Street between the Passaic River and the New Jersey Railroad to be used as a hospital after he learned about the high number of casualties in the Battle of Williamsburg, May 5, 1862. Ward was called the "soldier's friend" because he saw to it that the volunteers' monthly allowances were turned over to their families. His popularity led to his election as governor, serving from 1866 to 1869. Also, the Fairmount Cemetery set aside a plot for free burials for men who had served their nation. It was designated as the National Cemetery of Newark.

At the start of the war, Newark volunteers marched to ten waiting cars on the railroad for a ride to Trenton. At Trenton, they boarded ships for Washington via Chesapeake Bay, where they were inducted on May 6, 1861. It was the first fully-organized, fully-equipped brigade to reach the capital. Others followed rapidly, and in total, about 10,000 Newarkers served in the Civil War.

A draft law was signed by Abraham Lincoln in 1863. New Jersey avoided responding to it by voluntary enlistments that passed the state's assigned quota. The next year, however, the additional men were supplied by drafting. The units were trained in Military Park and quartered in Camp Frelinghuysen, located in the area of Branch Brook Park.

Major General Philip Kearny was known as "the One-Armed Devil" by the Confederate soldiers who both feared and respected him. Kearny commanded local forces in the Peninsula Campaign in Virginia until he was killed September 1, 1862, at Chantilly. Major General Philip Kearny, one of New Jersey's most famous leaders during the Civil War, was a native of New York City. He resided in Kearny Cottage on Broadway, later the site of the Newark Normal School. Kearny earned a law degree from Columbia in 1835, but enjoyed the excitement of the battlefield more than the courtroom. He lost his left arm in the Mexican War in 1848. A professional soldier, Kearny fought with Napoleon III at Solferino against the Austrians and with the French in the Algerian campaign. Returning home when the Civil War started, he took command of the First New Jersey Brigade. Kearny later commanded the Third Corps of the Army of Potomac and saw action in Williamsburg and Seven Pines.

The State of New Jersey commissioned Henry Kirke Browne to produce a statue of General Philip Kearny for Statuary Hall in Trenton. This statue was discovered in the basement of the building in 1879, and a committee of Newark citizens saw to it that the statue was installed and dedicated in Military Park in 1880. A sword that the general held disappeared a long time ago. A replica of the statue is located in Statuary Hall in Washington, D.C. The local officials of Kearny, named in his honor, also wanted to have the statue moved to its town. Authorities in the City of Newark disagreed, and another statue was found for the town. A bust of General Kearny also appears in the Metropolitan Museum of Art in New York City.

The Civil War was the first of the nation's military conflicts to be caught on camera. Nearly every soldier had small prints of photos of himself or his loved ones to carry to the battlefield or leave at home. Freelance photographers followed the troops and set up their tents on the edges of the battlefield to process film and

This is the much-disputed statue by Henry Kirke Browne honoring Philip Kearny, the Civil War hero.

This trolley car is seen passing a horse-drawn milk wagon. Note that the two vehicles take up one entire side of the street.

print photographs. Hundreds of photos were taken after the battles, showing the bodies of horses and men, the burned-out buildings, broken wagons, lost weapons, and neat rows of tents in the armies' campgrounds.

Horse cars, also called trolley cars, began appearing on the streets of Newark in 1859. The trolley cars were pulled by one or two horses. Although slow, they were faster than walking. Each trolley or group of trolleys was owned by an individual serving only a small section of the city. Each car was painted a different color from its competitors so that prospective passengers would know where the trolley was headed. The first of these was the Orange and Newark Horsecar Railroad. Additional street railroads formed quickly, and like the trains, they took people out of the city to the country to picnic, to enjoy the fresh air, to vacation, and finally to live. The cars also brought the country people to Newark to shop, work, or be entertained. The areas around Newark began to grow as people sought larger homes away from the factories with more land for their families.

The trolley cars were electrified in the 1890s and most of the companies were purchased by the Public Service Coordinated Transport, organized by Thomas N. McCarter Jr. in 1903. He suggested that the trolleys could use the Morris Canal bed to eliminate street traffic, but his idea was ignored. Trolley islands in the middle of Broad Street installed for the safety of the passengers for the trolleys became a hazard to motor vehicles as their numbers grew. Buses, though, were later favored over trolley cars because they could move anywhere on the street and get around obstacles.

An example of the trolley's danger, a tragic accident occurred on February 19, 1903, in which a train rammed a North Jersey Street Railway Company trolley car loaded with 120 persons, mostly students at Barringer High School. The motorman applied his brakes on a hill between Orange Street and the Lackawanna Railroad Tracks, but the brakes failed to hold. The trolley slid down the sloop through the gates into the path of the Bernardsville Special railroad train speeding to Newark. Nine persons were killed and 30 were injured. The Pennsylvania and the Jersey Central Railroads had already begun a program to eliminate grade crossings in Newark, but the Lackawanna had delayed action. Numerous lawsuits followed and the Lackawanna Railroad raised its tracks.

The Hudson and Manhattan Railroad Company was called the "Tubes," and it was started in 1908, when a tunnel was completed between New York and Jersey City. The road reached Newark in 1912. When the Pennsylvania Station was built in 1935, the third level was constructed for the "Tubes." Now known as PATH (Port Authority Trans Hudson Corporation) and operated by the Port Authority of New York and New Jersey, the trains run for 14 miles between Newark and New York City.

Up until 1903, there were dozens of little trolley and bus lines. Some of them only traveled a short distance. Like on the earlier horse cars, the passenger would have to dismount in all kinds of weather and wait for another bus or trolley car if there was one, or simply walk. Several vehicles might have to be taken to reach

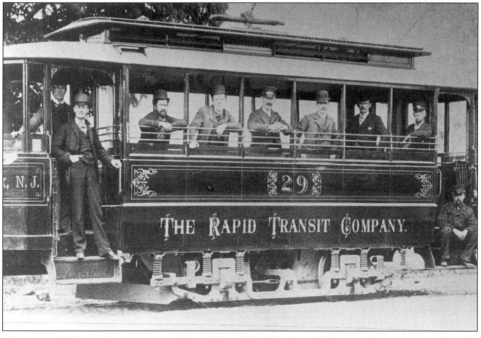

A group of fashionable passengers aboard Car 29 of the Rapid Transit Company pose for this early-twentieth-century photograph.

When the George Washington Bridge was opened on October 24, 1931, it gave Newarkers and other people another route into Manhattan Island. The tunnels and the bridge reduced travel time into New York City.

a destination only a few miles away. The unification of the routes by Public Service Transport made the ride more comfortable and efficient for the passengers. Most of these lines today are operated by New Jersey Transit, formed in 1983.

By 1914, jitney buses were carrying passengers along the streets of the city. These soon were replaced by buses. Gradually, these buses replaced the trolley lines. The last trolley car operated on Broad Street in December 1937, and the trolley islands were removed. Fortunately, the wires that supplied electricity for the trolleys had remained in place and when World War II began, the buses were altered to operate on electricity and use these lines as trolley-buses.

In the meantime, the Morris Canal bed in Newark was sold to the City in 1924. The City agreed to construct a subway if Public Service would operate and maintain it. The subway, actually a trolley, opened in 1935. It traveled between Penn Station and Franklin Street, Newark. Like other transportation vehicles in New Jersey, it is now operated by New Jersey Transit.

The canal and railroads brought produce to Newark and people to work in the new diverse manufacturing plants and stores. From the start, Newark was very diversified with leather goods, carriages and wagons, breweries, jewelry, hats, clothing, chemicals, boots and shoes, iron and steel, paints, and plastic products. With them came the need for insurance companies and banks, technical schools and colleges, recreational opportunities such as rowing clubs and ball fields, and houses of worship and ethnic associations to serve the new people from Europe, the South, and the countryside.

When the Holland Tunnel was opened on November 13, 1927, to carry traffic from Jersey City to New York City, it again reduced the travel time between Newark and New York City. It was a great boon to Newark. Before the tunnel, cars and trucks had to wait for ferries, which were delayed by storms—ice or snow. The tunnel was named for Clifford M. Holland, designer and first chief engineer of the tunnel. Full control of the tunnel was placed in the hands of the Port Authority in March 1931. The Lincoln Tunnel from Weehawken to New York City was completed in 1957, again assisting the movement of people, produce, and manufactured products.

The Pulaski Skyway, named for Polish General Casimir Pulaski, who assisted the American cause during the Revolutionary War, carries traffic for 3.5 miles above the Passaic and Hackensack Rivers and marshes, and when it opened in 1932, the route provided a traffic light–free ride. It was acclaimed America's outstanding highway project and was awarded first place in the beautiful bridge competition of the American Institute of Steel Construction.

The Pennsylvania Station was built in 1933–1935, and recently has been restored to its original Art Deco style with wall reliefs and ceiling sculptures. The 193-foot-high structure is finished in Indiana limestone. The Amtrak, Conrail, New Jersey Transit, and PATH trains use the station. The City Subway tracks run underneath the station, and there are two areas for local buses.

Cars and buses were allowed to pull up to the entrance of Pennsylvania Station, Newark, together in this photo taken in 1978.

The Newark Airport was begun in 1928, with a 1,600-foot asphalt runway, the first of its kind built for a commercial airport. The next year, the airport was designated as the metropolitan air mail terminus until 1935, when passenger service began. The airport was taken over by the government during World War II to export nearly 13 million tons of cargo for the war to the European and African Theaters from January 1942 to May 1945. Fighter planes were also flown from the airport, and gallons of aviation gas were shipped from Port Newark.

On March 11, 1948, the Port of New York Authority, now the Port Authority of New York and New Jersey, rented the airport from the City of Newark on a long-term lease. The Authority immediately began to improve and expand the airport into Elizabeth; Terminal A was built completely within the Union County city as were several auxiliary services at the airport. Today, it is considered to be the busiest in the New York area. Continental Airlines, which has a whole terminal at Newark International Airport, is Newark's largest employer.

Except for occasional noise complaints, which usually result in changes in landing and take-off procedures, the Newark International Airport has been a real boon to New Jersey. But in 1951–1952, within 56 days, 117 people in 3 airplanes and on the ground were killed in three crashes in Elizabeth. The first, on December 16, crashed into the Elizabeth River just east of Westfield Avenue. The second, on January 22, carrying former Secretary of War Robert P. Patterson, crashed near Battin High School in the rain. The third, on February 10, just

This small building at Newark International Airport (seen from the rear) was used as the administration building and passenger terminal for many years. The airport now has three enormous terminals to handle dozens of domestic and foreign flights.

Sailing ships were still in use as cargo ships as late as World War II. This undated photograph shows men working on a pier in Newark.

missed the Janet Memorial Home, an orphanage. The Port of New York Authority ordered the airport closed, and it was later reopened November 15, 1952, and has been opened ever since.

A monorail built in 1995 carries passengers to three terminals from the parking lots. These tracks have been extended for 1 mile to the new station to serve Amtrak and New Jersey Transit's Northeast Corridor commuter line on the mainline between Elizabeth and Newark. Passengers can reach the Newark City Subway at Pennsylvania Station.

Additional construction will take the monorail to Jersey Gardens, a shopping center in the Elizabeth meadows on the Arthur Kill, and to the Elizabeth station. One of the proposed stops will be at a new ferry line to operate to New York City. Ferry service from Elizabethport to New York City was initiated about 1990, but stopped because of lack of use. Meanwhile, the airport has expanded from a local field to one that services international carriers.

Eleven days after signing the lease for the airport, the Authority signed another lease for the seaport. Except for one or two cargo ships that carry passengers, Port Newark is primarily a cargo port—with automobiles being among its chief imports. The long-discussed mile-long channel from Newark Bay was dredged in 1915 just in time for supporting World War I in Europe. A second channel for Elizabeth was dredged nearby in 1958 for container ships. Dozens of containers are placed on tractor trailers every day at the port and driven to places throughout the country.

The Submarine Boat Company began building ships for the war effort in World War I at Port Newark. By January 1920, it had built a total of 52 ships, more than

Men work on a ship at the Submarine Boat Company during World War I. The boatyard was reactivated when World War II began.

any other port in that war. The federal government purchased the old Submarine Boat Company site in World War II for the Federal Shipbuilding Company, which constructed destroyers, destroyer escorts, troop and landing ships. The seaport shipped generators, vehicles, and other large articles to Europe for the war. The Weyerhauser Steamboat Company was the chief carrier, and several of its ships were lost in transit.

Newark is unique because the seaport, airport, Routes 1, 9, and 95, and the railroads are all within a stone's throw of each other, making it accessible to various forms of transportation. General George Washington was said to have been dismayed by the lack of roads and the poor conditions of the roads that were available during the late eighteenth century. Heeding his advice, Newark as a gateway city is constantly seeking to improve access to New Jersey as well as the states beyond it.

Route 29 (Route 22) was planned in 1927 to travel from Somerville to the junction of U.S. Highway 1 in Newark, passing through an old valley in Scotch Plains, Mountainside, Westfield, Springfield, Kenilworth, Union, and Hillside. Several variations were considered before the present route was selected. The work was finally completed and the highway, known as the Blue Star Highway, opened to Newark in 1933.

Newark's portion of Route 21 is called McCarter Highway, named for Uzal McCarter. The highway runs along the main line of the Pennsylvania Railroad tracks and runs parallel to the Passaic River nearly to Paterson.

Garden State Parkway, built for 172 miles by the New Jersey Highway Authority from the New York State border to Cape May, was opened in 1957, while the New Jersey Turnpike from the George Washington Bridge to the Delaware Memorial Bridge at Deepwater, 118 miles long, was constructed by the Turnpike Authority and opened in 1952. Both are toll roads. They carried people to the New Jersey shore and south or to the New York Thruway and north for recreation and new homes. The people of Newark followed these roads, and subdivisions appeared and New Jersey's famous farmland, which originally made it the Garden State, began to turn into suburbia. Strip malls grew to serve the new communities and were followed almost immediately by huge malls covering dozens of pastures.

Both Routes 280 and 78 slashed 1,000 feet or more through Newark just north and south of the central city, destroying homes and apartments of thousands of people who either moved to other sections of the city or out of the city in the 1960s. More housing was destroyed when the college, now the University of Medicine and Dentistry, started buying property around the Martland Hospital on Bergen Street for the new school at the same time.

Route 280 was contemplated as early as 1930, but it was not until the year 1973 before it was opened between Route 80 at Parsippany–Troy Hills and Harrison. Construction, which started in 1964, cut through First and Second Mountains and bridged the Passaic River. The construction threatened the House of Prayer and Plume House, one of the oldest dwellings in the city.

Taking longer to construct, Route 78 was started in 1957. The highway was completed from Phillipsburg to Berkeley Heights, a distance of 38 miles, by 1976. It was halted by a 5-mile area through the Watchung Reservation by oppositions by the officials of Union County and conservationists. In its path was the Deserted Village, which Union County parks is restoring, and Surprise Lake. In addition to the reservation, the original plans for the highway to cut through residential areas of Springfield, Union, and Hillside Townships were opposed by the townships' local governments and the people alike. Compromises were reached. The 63-mile-long highway, completed in 1986, skirted the reservation and a Springfield park, cut through a residential section of Union, and followed the Hillside-Irvington border.

Transportation turned Newark from a sleepy, little hamlet into the largest municipality in New Jersey. But people could go both ways. The improved roads took people out of the city to the countryside, where new suburbs developed. In 1940, just before World War II, the population of Newark was recorded at 429,760. The war introduced many young men and women in the service to the opportunities of the world.

In 1950, when the men and women returned home, 438,776 people were counted, the highest number ever tallied in Newark's population. Years of Depression and war had curbed construction of housing units. Industrialists who had made do in outmoded nineteenth-century factories for the war effort wanted new facilities and the City lacked land for these improvements or additions. The

A container is lifted from a tractor at dockside and is being placed on a container ship. Port Newark–Port Elizabeth has become one of the largest container ship facilities in the world.

industrialists wanted non-union labor and that was hard to find in Newark, a strong labor environment.

The returned servicemen looked for homes in the new suburbs. Demolition of houses for roads, the medical school, and colleges continued to remove more people. By 1980, the population had decreased to 329,248. In 1990, it had fallen to 275,221, and the census for the new century is given as only 273,546 people. Left behind were people with low incomes who believed they were unable to afford the suburbs or African Americans who were unwelcomed in the new all-white neighborhoods.

The new roads also caused the development of huge shopping and strip malls. City department stores, grocery stores, and chain stores began to close as they followed the population to the malls. New office buildings were built near the malls, and doctors, lawyers, and other professionals moved to them. Bus and train service decreased. The automobile had changed the way people of Newark lived, worked, and played. Against a tradition of mass transit, the automobile had become king.

The improvements in transportation—better roads, ferries, bridges, the Morris Canal, trains, "Tubes," seacraft, and finally aircraft—made Newark the transportation hub of New Jersey, as well as much of the East Coast. Transportation helped to make Newark the center of commerce, industry, education, and culture in New Jersey; it also helped the people to move beyond the mountains.

5. The Movers and Shakers

Newark is fortunate in having a long list of outstanding people. The first two ministers, Reverend Abraham Pierson Sr. and Jr., established the theocracy despite the presence of the Proprietors. Reverend Pierson Sr. disapproved of the Half Way Covenant in Connecticut and he was faced with the hostile Proprietors in Newark, who declared that only they had the right to distribute land.

Reverend Pierson supervised the building of the town's first meeting house. Seats were assigned by office, age, estate, infirmity, descent, or parentage. The deacons had the best seats. An hour glass was situated beside the Bible to measure the time, and the code for behavior for all was strict.

During the week, Reverend Pierson visited the homes of his parishioners whenever there was an emergency, and he kept a protective eye on the town's ordinances. Although he was only 54 years old when he came to Newark, he grew weaker, and on August 9, 1678 (at age 65), he died. He left a library of 440 books, one of the largest private collections in the colonies.

His son, Reverend Abraham Pierson Jr., was approved as his assistant as he grew older and succeeded him in the pulpit when he died. The younger Pierson was the first clergyman to be born in the colonies. He was recognized for his intellect, but criticized by some for his independence on church rites. He had been promised 80 pounds a year from his parishioners, but some withheld the fee. Others also wanted to withdraw the promise of firewood. Both were granted, but by then Reverend Pierson had accepted a call to a church in Killingworth in the Connecticut Colony, and after 10 years, he became rector of the College of Connecticut, now Yale University. He died in 1706.

The Piersons were followed by several pastors, none of whom served very long. The second meeting house, which was burned during the Revolutionary War, was built about 1713, when Newark was incorporated by Queen Anne of England. Four years later, the church became a Presbyterian affiliate when it joined the Presbytery of Philadelphia.

Governor Jonathan Belcher, then living in Elizabethtown in the Belcher-Ogden House, now owned by the Elizabethtown Historical Foundation, introduced the concept of the separation of church and town. In the past, the people of Newark voted on the preacher's salary and firewood supply at a town meeting. On June 5, 1753, Governor Belcher granted a new charter separating them. The church would have to provide for the pastor's needs, not the town.

Reverend Aaron Burr Sr., who is more famous for his son's misdeeds than his own achievements, became the president of the College of New Jersey (later Princeton University) after the death of Reverend Jonathan Dickinson, the founding president, in 1747, at Elizabethtown. The college was temporarily moved to Burr's parsonage in Newark.

Burr resigned his pulpit in 1755 to devote his full time and attention to the college. The trustees of the college wanted its location closer to Philadelphia. They estimated that there should be 10 acres of cleared ground and 200 acres of woodland. They wanted to place the school in New Brunswick, which failed to respond. Princeton did, and the building was started in 1753. The trustees wanted to name it for Governor Belcher. He, in turn, recommended Nassau Hall for William III, Prince of Orange-Nassau, and Nassau Hall it became.

Governor Jonathan Belcher recommended that the building at the College of New Jersey be called Nassau Hall, and it later became part of the Battle of Princeton on January 3, 1777.

Reverend Aaron Burr Sr. moved the College of New Jersey to Princeton when he was president of the institution.

The Burrs moved to Princeton when the building was completed. Unfortunately, the senior Burr died in September 1757 at 41 years of age. His last formal act as a minister was to preach at the funeral of Governor Belcher in Elizabethtown earlier that month. His wife, Esther Edwards Burr, died a few months later, leaving two parentless children, Sally and Aaron Jr. Mrs. Burr's father, Reverend Jonathan Edwards, who was noted for his fiery sermons, followed his son-in-law as president of Princeton. It became Princeton University in 1890.

Aaron Burr Jr. was educated at the Academy in Elizabethtown and the College of New Jersey. He won praise for his service during the Revolutionary War and was vice-president of the United States under President Thomas Jefferson. He and Alexander Hamilton clashed and finally agreed to meet at Weehawken for a dual in 1804. Hamilton is said not to have aimed at Burr, while Burr's shot killed Hamilton. He then became involved in several land schemes in the West. However, he was tried and found innocent.

The Schuylers, who actually lived across the Passaic River from Newark, usually were identified as being Newarkers. Colonel Peter Schuyler led men from Newark north in 1757 to face the French at Oswego, New York, in the French and Indian Wars. The men were captured and imprisoned at Montreal. They all were released in 1758. Other marches were led by Schuyler in 1759 and 1760. Peace came in 1763.

Reverend Dr. Alexander Macwhorter became pastor of the First Presbyterian Church in 1759, and he was an outspoken critic of the British. In 1776, during Washington's famous retreat, Reverend Macwhorter had to leave the town to escape the British, and his life continued to be in danger throughout the war. After the conflict, Reverend Macwhorter helped rebuild the destroyed church and remained the pastor of the congregation until his death in 1807.

Dr. William Burnet, a surgeon and an Elizabethtown native, warned Newarkers in 1776 to move their herds, grains, carriages, and other valuables out of Newark to escape the approaching British army. Dr. Burnet conducted hospitals in the villages, two churches, and the Newark Academy. David Gouverneur Burnet, one of his 11 children, became the first president of the *ad interim* government of early Texas in 1836.

Elisha Boudinot was the younger brother of Elias Boudinot, president of the Continental Congress. He and his wife, Catherine Smith, settled in a house on Park Place after their Elizabethtown marriage. Elisha, a lawyer and judge, was active in the various committees to fight the Revolutionary War. The Boudinot brothers were among the French Huguenots whose families fled to England and then to the colonies. Boudinot was selected to be the host for Marquis de Lafayette on his final trip to the United States in 1824, when he visited Newark.

Washington Irving, the writer, was a frequent visitor at the Gouverneur Mansion on the Passaic River. He called it "Cockloft Hall" instead of Mount Pleasant. It was adjacent to the site of the future Mount Pleasant Cemetery on Broadway. Irving resided at the mansion for some time with some young friends and is said to have written the *Salmagundi Papers* there. Ichabod Crane in the "Legend of Sleepy Hollow" may have been based on a New Jerseyan. Irving Street in nearby Rahway was named for his family, who resided there for sometime.

Washington Irving was a guest at Isaac Kemble's Cockloft Hall, located above the Passaic River in the vicinity of today's Mount Pleasant Avenue and Gouverneur Street.

Mayor William Halsey, the first mayor of the City of Newark, had more than his share of problems when he took the helm of the 37,000-person city. He worked to improve safety on the streets, to establish a fire department, to find quarters for the city government, and to better the water supply.

William Halsey, one of the welcoming party for Lafayette, was elected first mayor of the City of Newark in 1836 and found himself with a host of problems. There were complaints about the crowd at the city market blocking the street, the need for a larger night watch, a place to meet, a new jail, and a better water supply.

The Central Market was moved from Market Street to Mulberry Street and placed on top of the Morris Canal. The problem of a meeting place was solved by sharing quarters in the new Essex County Court House building for 10 years. Also, more men were hired to keep people from gathering on the streets at night.

One improvement resulted from embarrassment of the city fathers in April 1852, when Louis Kossuth, the Hungarian patriot, visited the city. The visit followed a heavy rain storm, and a wagon in the parade to welcome the visitor collapsed, throwing its occupants into the mud. A horse frightened by the noise reared, throwing its rider into the mud. A trumpeter interrupted the speech of welcome by proclaiming the arrival of "King Mud" and a scow was pulled down the street causing waves of mud to splash on each side. The street was paved a short time later.

William A. Whitehead was responsible for bringing the year-old New Jersey Historical Society from Trenton in 1846 to Newark, where it has been ever since. Whitehead also established the Newark Library Association, which sold stock to raise money to purchase books. Books were free to members, but cost $2 a year

Frederick Theodore Frelinghuysen served in many different leadership roles: state attorney general, senator, secretary of state, trustee of Rutgers, and president of the American Bible Society.

for non-members. Two years later, the library association was able to move into a stone building on Market Street. Whitehead encouraged it to rent the top floor to the historical society and one of the stores on the first floor to the post office and the other to an insurance company. The building, with an auditorium large enough to seat 700 people, was rented to the Fifth Presbyterian Church on Sundays and the Common Council for meetings. Whitehead was secretary and president of the library from 1851 to 1884 and also secretary of the state historical society. He was also a member of the Newark Board of Education and a trustee at Newark Academy and the Newark Normal School. The library association was dissolved in 1888, when the Free Public Library was incorporated.

Theodore Frelinghuysen (1789–1862), a member of the fourth generation of an early Dutch family, served in the United States Senate, as attorney general of New Jersey, president of Rutgers University from 1850 to 1862, mayor of Newark in 1837 and 1838, and ran unsuccessfully with Henry Clay on the Whig party ticket for President of the United States in 1844.

Frelinghuysen had no children of his own, so he adopted his nephew, Frederick Theodore Frelinghuysen (1817–1885), an abolitionist, who also became a lawyer. Frederick served as Newark City attorney in 1849 and as a member of the Newark City Council in 1850. He was appointed to the United States Senate in 1866 and was elected in 1871, serving until 1877. Under President Lincoln, Frelinghuysen served as the United States attorney general and then secretary of state under

President Chester A. Arthur. The recruitment camp in Branch Brook Park during the Civil War was named Camp Frelinghuysen in his honor. A statue of Frelinghuysen by Karl Gerhard was unveiled in Military Park in 1904. His son, Frederick (1848–1924), served as the president of the Howard Savings Institution and the Mutual Benefit Life Insurance Company.

Newark has provided several governors to New Jersey besides Marcus L. Ward and Franklin Murphy. William Sanford Pennington, a Democrat, served from 1812 to 1813, while his son, William, a Whig, was governor from 1837 to 1843, and selected as Speaker of the House of Representatives in 1860. Both Penningtons were abolitionists. The first Pennington issued a proclamation in July 1814 for the militia to serve in the War of 1812, but hostilities ended before any local troops entered combat.

Marcus Ward, who was elected governor after the Civil War, was known as the "soldier's friend" because he went out of his way to assist those who served and were wounded. Ward established a hospital in a building near the Passaic River and a home for disabled soldiers in Newark after the war. As president of the Board of Trade, he spearheaded the city's first industrial exposition, which he opened in 1872.

New Jersey governor Marcus Ward was known as the "soldier's friend" because of his efforts to assist the men who served in the Civil War.

Stephen Crane, the ninth child of Reverend and Mrs. Jonathan Townley Crane, showed unusual promise as a writer of poetry, nonfiction, and fiction in a career that spanned about 10 years.

Mayor Thomas Lynch Raymond, for whom Raymond Boulevard is named, was a man of vision. He encouraged the formation of the Newark Airport on the swamps and the development of Newark's port, recruited young men for the war effort in World War I, and sought a clean water supply for the city.

Edward I. Koch, former mayor of New York City, resided near South Side High School from the time he was 7 years old until he was 17. His father, a furrier, had lost his business during the Depression and joined his uncle's catering business on Belmont Avenue. Ed and his brother checked coats when they were youngsters. Later, Ed delivered groceries for a local deli.

Stephen Crane shook up the literary world with his handful of novels. His stories and books are described as naturalistic and realistic. When other writers of his day romanticized war, especially the Civil War, his acclaimed *Red Badge of Courage* did not, while his *Maggie, Girl of the Streets* accurately depicted the hard life of a young prostitute in New York City. Born in Newark and the son and grandson of ministers, he was an indifferent student. He joined his brother, Jonathan Townley Crane Jr., in Asbury Park, where he operated a news collection service and worked as a reporter. Later, he went to Florida to report on the Spanish-American War and then to Greece to write about a war there. He died at 29 in Baden, Germany, of tuberculosis and he is buried in Evergreen Cemetery on the Newark-Hillside line. His writing changed the way many subjects, such as war, were treated in novels in the twentieth century and continues to shape the visions and voices of contemporary writers.

Josephine Lawrence, author of a book column in the *Newark Evening News* for many years, wrote some 22 novels and many short stories mostly dealing with the Newark experience.

Philip Roth, a Newark native, who grew up in the Weequahic section, uses his hometown as the setting for many of his novels. His first novel, *Goodbye, Columbus*, based on his experiences in Weequahic High School, became a motion picture, and his work was awarded the National Book Award in 1959. He was awarded the Pulitzer Prize for his 1997 novel, *American Pastoral*, in which he used the nickname of another Newarker, "Swede," for his hero. The "Swede" was a member of the Class of 1938, who received the nickname at a summer camp for his height, blond hair, and blue eyes. His real name was Seymour Masin and he was an all-around athlete, playing basketball and football and competing in track. Later, he became a liquor salesman. A special display of Roth's work and photographs of Newark scenes were featured in France in 1999.

Newark introduced several other nationally celebrated writers onto the literary scene of twentieth-century America. Author Zane Gray, whose stories of the West pleased generations of readers, was born in the Ironbound section of Newark. Louis Ginsburg, an English teacher in the Paterson schools and a poet, and his son, Allen (Ginsberg), known as the famous Beat poet, were both born in Newark. Hannah Litzky, an English teacher at Weequahic High School, was Louis's sister.

Dore Schary, who honed his skills at the Newark YM-YWHA, was multi-talented. He wrote several books, including two about Thomas A. Edison, one on Boys Town, an autobiography, and a novel about special occasions—maybe based on the activities of his father's banquet hall in Newark. Schary also wrote Broadway plays, and the most outstanding and celebrated was *Sunrise at Campobello*. He was a screenwriter in the 1920s, an executive producer, and finally vice president in charge of production at MGM Studios from 1948 to 1956.

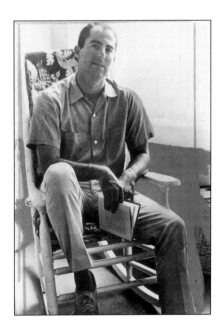

One of Newark's most recognized writers is Philip Roth, who was awarded the Pulitzer Prize for his novel American Pastoral.

The John Ballantine Mansion, a 17-room residence designed by George Edward Harney, was restored by the Newark Museum.

John Cotton Dana served as the library director from 1902 to 1929. Dana is responsible for making the present beautiful building at 5 Washington Street a first-class library. Students of library science would spend a year or so working with him to be better trained in their assigned libraries.

The Ballantine family is another name that became well known in Newark. Peter Ballantine started a brewery and his three sons followed him into the business. The house of Peter's son John is part of the Newark Museum. The house was designed by George Edward Harney and took two years, from 1883 to 1885, to build. It is a blend of Renaissance and Romanesque Revival styles. The panels around the top of the porch and front bay window are carved with floral and foliate designs The grey granite porch columns have carved Corinthian capitals. The house has a modified mansard roof with gabled dormers. The flat facade is typical of a city rowhouse. The interior features cherry, ash, maple, and mahogany wood. Each fireplace had a different variety and color of English ceramic tile and wooden mantel. The house had stained-glass windows and ornamented ceilings. Some of the walls were hung in moire or damask. The 17-room mansion was staffed by 16 live-in servants. The house was sold in 1920 to the Commercial Casualty Insurance Company, which used it for offices until the museum purchased it in 1937. The Rutgers Law School used it briefly after World War II before the old residence was incorporated into the museum.

Louis Bamberger and his brother-in-law, Felix Fuld, purchased a small store and turned it into a merchandising giant offering all types of goods. Prior to the opening of L. Bamberger & Company, L.S. Plaut and Hahne's stores had specialized in one product. This new general approach was successful and Bamberger and Fuld became the chief benefactors of Newark. Bamberger assisted the Newark Museum, while Mrs. Fuld, Louis's sister, donated the famous cherry trees to Branch Brook Park.

Prohibition brought bootleggers to Newark. There were several, but the one who was most outstanding was Abner "Longy" Zwillman. On one hand, Zwillman was bringing illegal liquor into the city and distributing it and accumulating several legitimate businesses; on the other hand, in the depths of the Depression, he served as a Robin Hood figure to the poor Jewish population in the old Third Ward, distributing food and meeting their needs.

Mrs. Parker O. Griffith, wife of the owner of the Griffith Piano Company and the Griffith Building on Broad Street, arranged concerts, operas, and ballets at the old Mosque Theater on Broad Street from the 1920s to 1958, when the Griffith Foundation cancelled its season. The performers, mostly attached to New York companies, appeared at more nominal admission to make their performances available to everyone.

Louis Bamberger purchased a failed store and turned it into the successful L. Bamberger & Company by offering a variety of products under one roof.

Dr. Reynold E. Burch and his wife, Mary, organized the Leaguers in 1950.

Jerry Lewis, who was Joseph Levitch when he attended South Side High School, became the clown of clowns. In 1957, he became the national chairman of the Muscular Dystrophy Association and continues to raise funds for it each year on Labor Day in a nationwide telethon.

George Kahn of the YM-YWHA created the *Bits of Hits* show, segments from Broadway shows at the Y. He encouraged local talent such as Fanny Brice to appear at the Y, while inviting promising performers from New York. He presented plays by Moss Hart and Dore Schary and music by Jerome Kern. Harry Friedgut arranged lectures by outstanding speakers. During World War II, Kahn prepared programs at camps and hospitals for servicemen.

William M. Ashby, when a youth, lived in Roselle and commuted to school in Newark to become a social worker and supported himself by working in Newark restaurants as a busboy. He formed the Urban Leagues in both Elizabeth and Newark, starting in 1916, to improve the plight of the Southern rural African-American population that had moved north for a better life. A quiet man and always a gentleman, he persistently and insistently fought against racial prejudices and attempted to improve the African Americans' living conditions.

In 1950, Dr. Reynold E. Burch and his wife, Dr. Mary B. Burch, formed the Leaguers Educational Cultural Youth Program at 731 Clinton Avenue in the Clinton Hill section to assist African-American youths. The program included a head start for pre-schoolers, tutorial assistance for schoolchildren, college scholarships, after-school care, youth programs, summer day camp, life skills, community development projects, an early childhood development center, and a variety of social activities, including debutante balls and reunions for people who have been members.

Dionne Warwick, the singer-actress, is the Leaguers most famous alumna and she received her first college scholarship at the 1959 cotillion. Miss Warwick told an interviewer, "I don't know where I would be today if it weren't for Mrs. Burch and the Leaguers." Mrs. Burch was a member of the board of trustees of Kean University and a founder of Essex County College and was the first African-American woman on the Newark Board of Education.

Right Reverend Monsignor William Linder, pastor of St. Rose of Lima Roman Catholic Church, spearheaded the formation of the New Community Corporation (NCC) program in 1968, when he conducted a survey of the parishioners of Queen of Angels Roman Catholic Church in the Central Ward, where he was assigned as a priest, to discover what they needed most. The parishioners answered that they needed good housing, child care, and jobs. Linder sought to solve their problems. The results were a non-profit housing corporation with recreational programs for children and adults, special classes in conjunction with the Springfield Avenue Branch of the Newark Public Library, low- and middle-income housing, and a supermarket.

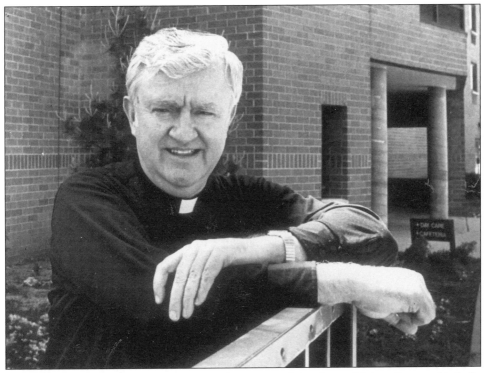

Right Reverend Monsignor William Linder, pastor of St. Rose of Lima Roman Catholic Church, is pictured in front of some buildings erected by New Community Corporation.

The Youth Consultation Service on Broadway serves troubled youth. It was built as the Protestant Foster Home by the Episcopal Diocese in 1875 for orphans.

The facilities varied from apartments to town houses to garden apartments. The most recent town homes are being sold to the occupants. Other services included job placement, job training, credit union, health services, medical day care, two charter schools, an early learning center, and an alternative school. All maintenance and security personnel are hired from among the residents of the New Community Corporation.

Richard Grossklaus and David Kerr at first organized a social club in Belleville for recovering drug addicts. In 1968, they acquired a house formerly owned by Richard Hahne, the department store owner at Lincoln Park, rehabilitated it, and formed Integrity Inc., a community of concerned people working together to help themselves and each other by changing each individual's lifestyle. They continued to purchase property, and with the assistance of their clients, they restored the land around Lincoln Park and kept the park clean. Since they began, Integrity Inc. has assisted some 18,000 drug addicts.

Under the leadership of Stephen Adubato Sr., the North Ward Educational and Cultural Center at 346 Mt. Prospect Avenue uses the former Clark mansion, built in 1880, to provide daycare for children and recreational programs for youth and adults. The Youth Consultation Service at 284 Broadway uses the former Protestant Foster Home, built in 1875, to assist troubled youth.

Aspira, a Hispanic group, seeks to teach persons with a Hispanic heritage the English language and how to cope in this society. Individual churches and groups assisting drug addicts also are in the city offering help. There are many soup kitchens to assist the homeless, jobless, or those with below poverty level incomes.

Raymond Chambers, a philanthropist, is the person behind the construction of the New Jersey Performing Arts Center and the Bears & Eagles Riverfront Stadium. A Newark native from a modest family, he accumulated wealth and is returning it to the city he loves.

Two of the many local leaders who are are interested in revitalizing the city include Michael Skurnick, chief financial officer of Cogswell Realty Group, Manhattan, which has restored the National Newark and Essex Bank Building at 744 Broad Street and the Lefcourt Building on Commerce Street; and Charles Kushner, president of Kushner Cos. of Florham Park, who purchased the 20-story Mutual Benefit Life Insurance Company Building opposite Washington Park on Broad Street and rented it to IDT Corporation, a telecommunications company for 15 years. He also has purchased another office building at 60 Park Place.

John Petrillo, chairman of New Newark Foundation (NNF), purchased 24 parcels of land around the old Hahne & Company building, which NNF hopes to turn into an area of apartments, ground-level retail shops, restaurants, nightclubs, and galleries. Jerome Gottesman, president of Edison Properties Inc., operated some 150 parking lots. The company owns 6.2 acres in the center of the

Assemblyman Michael Adubato administers the oath of office to his nephew, Assemblyman Stephen Adubato Jr. as Mildred Adubato, mother of Michael and grandmother of Stephen, watches in 1984.

In 1967, Kenneth Gibson, a civil engineer, served as the first African-American mayor of Newark.

40-acre plot selected for the Devils-Nets arena in the former Chinatown section of Newark. If the arena is built, it will house the New Jersey Devils hockey team and the Nets basketball team. In addition, Edison Properties Inc. has signed an agreement with Leslie Smith Jr., senior vice president of the Rockefeller Group Development, to build a 22-story office building along the Passaic River near Penn Station.

Miles Berger, president of the Berger Hotels Corporation, owns the Robert Treat Hotel and plans to demolish the Lincoln Motel, a welfare hotel, and replace it with an office and residential development. Mayor Sharpe James, who also is a state senator, has directed the clean-up and fencing of vacant city lots, which became dumping grounds for tires, garbage, and other debris. The streets are well lighted and swept regularly. Flowers and ornamental bushes have been planted throughout the city and festive flags hang from lampposts. Mayor James also actively seeks builders for more than 200 vacant city lots

Newark has had many people of good will who seek to make Newark and the world around them better. Some have chosen religion, education, or elected offices. Several have founded or operated local organizations and some write, perform, or simply create art. These different men and women of Newark have dared to be innovative, different, and forceful, working hard to achieve what they think is worth doing for the good of all. The city and the people who live and work in it benefit from their tireless efforts.

6. SCHOOL DAYS

Newarkers have always been interested in education. On October 31, 1676, the provincial authorities granted Newark permission to open a school. There is no further mention of the school, and it may have been conducted at the meeting house, the normal place to conduct all community events. After being hired, the schoolmaster would be assigned to board with various members of the congregation.

The first documented school in present-day Newark's city limits apparently was the Lyon's Farms School, built in 1728, on the Upper Road to Elizabethtown at Pot Pie Lane. Residents dropped the possessive apostrophe with usage and it became Lyons Farms. This school was once a one-room structure and was apparently free to local citizens. There is no record that the parents paid, while all the other early schools in this time period usually charged tuition fees.

When General George Washington made his famous retreat from Fort Lee to Washington's Crossing, the children of the Lyons Farms School gathered in front of the school to wave to him. When the British and Hessian troops followed, the children reportedly hid in the bushes and behind the trees nearby. The school was used briefly as a hospital during the war and then burned by the British invaders.

The structure was rebuilt in 1784 from stone cut at a quarry up Pot Pie Lane (Chancellor Avenue). The school building was used until 1902. In 1938, the school was moved by the Works Progress Administration to the Newark Museum garden, where it stands today, at the suggestion of Dr. William R. Ward Jr.

Also in early Newark, Reverend Aaron Burr Sr., pastor of the Presbyterian Church from 1737 to 1755, conducted classes in his manse. In 1776, a school for white children was conducted on Market Street.

The Newark Academy was founded in 1774 and used a building on the Upper Common, now Washington Park. It opened for instruction on April 3, 1775. It is the sixth-oldest private boys' school in the nation. Both students and

Three faculty members of Newark Academy stand with the Class of 1884, numbering only 25 members.

schoolmaster boarded in the building when it was opened. Reading, writing, arithmetic, and bookkeeping became its chief subjects, although it initially was called the Latin Grammar School.

Its first schoolmaster, William Haddon, fled when the Revolution's hostilities began and joined the British. The school building was used as a barracks, guardhouse, and hospital until January 25, 1780, when it was burned after 15 Continental soldiers, asleep inside, were arrested. The militiamen were taken to prison in New York City.

Efforts to rebuild the academy began in 1791, with a meeting at Gifford's Tavern. After the war, the academy was rebuilt under the leadership of a committee, including Reverend Dr. Alexander Macwhorter, pastor of the Presbyterian Church, and Reverend Uzal Ogden, rector of the Trinity Church. Abraham Ogden and Elisha Boudinot were appointed two years later to petition the state legislature to permit a lottery to raise 800 pounds to rebuild the academy. A lot on Broad Street at Academy Street was purchased and St. John's Lodge, F. & A.M., was given exclusive use of the upper floor in appreciation for the funds it contributed to the construction. James Moffet, a native of Scotland, became the first teacher in 1792 in the new building.

For a time after 1808, Newark Academy was coeducational. Then, a Miss Van Doren ran a school for a while in the Newark Academy building, which Lafayette visited in 1824. The school later returned to a boys-only educational institution. After 1816, instruction was offered to wage earners from 5:30 to 7:30 a.m. daily, except on Sundays. Dancing classes also were offered in the summer, with practice balls at the Jersey Tavern. The school's leaders purchased the Wesleyan Institute on High Street in the 1850s. Its last home in Newark was on First Street at William Street before the school moved to Livingston in 1964, when the trustees realized that most of the students, 80 percent, lived beyond the city's limits. A stone with a plaque was dedicated during the 250th anniversary of the settlement of Newark on the spot where the academy originally stood. The cost was paid by the trustees, teachers, graduates, and students at the academy. In 1968, the school became coed and continues to be coed today.

Another private school, the White School, was established in 1797 by Captain Jabez Parkhurst. Three other academies were formed in the next decade: the Market Street School in 1804, the Franklin School (on Fair Street) in 1807, and the Union School (on New Street) in 1809. In 1815, the town allocated money for schooling for poor children.

Public schools were started by order of state law in 1829, but a state board of education to supervise these schools was not established until 1867, and Newark's board of education was formed in 1851. Four free schools were opened by the City of Newark in 1836, the year the community became a city. A revision in the state's 1844 constitution in 1875 directed that free schools be provided for all children between the ages of 5 and 18 years. This is the same year that the state adopted a statute giving all African-American men the right to vote and removed the word "white" from the state constitutional requirements for voting.

This is an 1860 diploma from Newark's first high school, Newark Public High School.

Photographed by William F. Cone, the Newark High School required new facilities due to the increase in the number of students.

Despite the free education, some people preferred to continue to send their children to private schools or have a private tutor because they thought of free schools as schools for the poor. Some of the poor children were sent to private schools paid for with city funds. Many of the public classes met in church basements, usually heatless and damp.

Newark's first high school was opened in 1839. This public institution was known as the Newark High School until it was renamed for William Barringer, first superintendent of schools. Its first location was in a building formerly used as a private school. Originally, the school only catered to boys' education, for another site had been founded to teach the girls.

In a more personal story, Barringer on a visit to the home of the superintendent of schools in Elizabeth made a point of kissing his mother-in-law, a D'Anterroches. Barringer explained that he wanted to kiss the woman who had been kissed by Marquis de Lafayette, her cousin. She was a child when Lafayette visited her family's home in Elizabethtown as the nation's guest on his grand tour in 1824.

A new school was built for Barringer High School near Branch Brook Park in 1899. In 1872, commercial subjects were added to its curriculum. Barringer, the superintendent of schools, urged the state to pass an industrial education law in 1881. A school was opened in 1884 on West Park Street. Classes were conducted for three hours nightly. Students attended from three to five years before graduating. The school moved to High Street six years later and began holding day classes also. In 1896, a new building was erected and named for Edward

Weston, a benefactor. It became the Newark Technical School and in 1919, Newark College of Engineering. Since 1975, it has been the New Jersey Institute of Technology.

John Whitehead realized the poor conditions of the schools needed improvement and went to the city council seeking new independent buildings. Whitehead arranged a tour of the existing schools for the city council, and they were impressed with his argument. The result was the construction of three schools: State, Commerce, and Market Streets in 1847–1848. Three additional schools were erected in 1851, and the "colored" school met in the basement of the African Presbyterian Church in Plane Street. The new high school building on Washington and Linden Streets opened in January 1855. Newark finally was on its way to becoming the best school system in New Jersey.

Evening classes were conducted for adults, boy apprentices, and others who worked during the day. Child labor laws were not adopted until 1884, when the minimum age for working was set at 12 years for boys and 14 for girls. The laws unfortunately were not enforced, and young children were still used in the mills because they could get behind the machinery more easily. In 1904, the child labor law raised the working age for boys to 14 years and set a maximum of 10 hours a day and a 55-hour work week in mines and factories.

Eberhardt Hall, at 323 King Boulevard, was built in 1857 as the Newark Orphan Asylum. It became the Newark Technical School and then the Newark College of Engineering in 1919. Today, it is the New Jersey Institute of Technology.

The desire for education especially on the part of the adults caused the Newark Library Association to be formed in 1845. A three-story building was erected on Market Street, and the third floor was rented to the New Jersey Historical Society, formed a year earlier in Trenton. The first floor contained stores that were rented for income. A lecture hall to seat 700 people was located on the second floor for public meetings, including the city council, the Fifth Presbyterian Church on Sundays, and for other special events. The library was opened nightly, and there were even complaints that too many apprentices gathered in it.

The library moved to the Park Theater on West Park Street in 1889. Plans were made for a new library building, which was constructed in 1901, on Washington Street by Frank Hill, the librarian. John Cotton Dana, the most famous librarian, spearheaded the founding of the Newark Museum on the fourth floor in 1909. Dana also started a separate business branch library in 1904, which was relocated at the main library in 1995. Foreign language books were added to the collection to serve non-English–speaking residents.

The Newark Normal School was established by an act of the state legislature in 1855, along with Trenton and Paterson as two-year teachers' training schools. The course work was increased to three years in 1928, and by 1934, it was a four-year college granting a bachelor's degree as the Newark State Teachers College. The college moved to Union Township in 1958 and changed its name to Kean College to honor U.S. Senator Hamilton Fish Kean, on whose former estate the 120-acre university is located; it became Kean University in 1995.

This is the ornate doorway to the two-year Newark Normal School.

The Franklin School was one of the early elementary schools in Newark.

By 1860, before the Civil War began, there was 1 public high school, the Newark High School, 10 grammar schools, 11 primary schools, 3 primary industrial schools, 5 evening schools (4 for males and 1 for females), 1 Saturday morning normal school, and 1 school for "colored" children.

The first night high school started in 1890. Day schools were overcrowded despite the fact that many children were never enrolled or if enrolled, never bothered to attend. New schools were built. The population between 1900 and 1910 increase by 100,000 people. More schools were needed. Children by law were forced to stay in school until they were 14. Earlier, boys could leave at 12. Fifteen more schools were erected in a four-year period.

The Central Commercial and Manual Training High School on High Street (Martin Luther King Boulevard) opened in 1912. The next year, South Side High in South Newark and East Side Commercial and Manual Training School in the Ironbound section opened. Fifteen grammar schools also were completed in this period to meet the growing demand caused by population increases.

The Arts High School opened in the 1920s for those children skilled in art and music. In order to qualify for admission, they underwent tests to show proficiency. Tests were and still are given to children before their admission in Science High School in the building used by Newark University, Public Service, and Ballantine Beer. The West Kinney Alternative High School in 1985 began a program for students who dropped out or had problems such as pregnancy and emotional and neurological impairments. Gateway Academy began in 1998 for teenagers who were on parole or probation.

Dr. Alma Flagg, teacher, assistant superintendent, and poet, was honored by having a school named after her in the Roseville section.

Bragaw Avenue School was built when Maple Avenue School became overcrowded. Its annex on Chancellor Avenue became Floyd Patterson High School in honor of the heavyweight champion in May 1980. The school was set up to teach socially maladjusted students from 14 to 21 years of age.

In 1985, a new school in the Roseville section of the city was named the Dr. E. Alma Flagg School in honor of Dr. Flagg, a retired assistant superintendent of schools. Dr. Flagg, who is also a poet, served as secretary for the Newark Landmarks and Preservation Committee for many years. Her husband, Dr. Thomas Flagg, also a Newark teacher, became a professor at Montclair State College. Both their children have become educators.

The influx of immigrants to the city after the Civil War increased the interest in education. Classes in English as a second language were taught at night to Italian and Jewish immigrants who were eager to communicate with their neighbors in their new country and find good employment. There also was instruction in the "basics," such as reading and arithmetic because many of the immigrants had had little, if any, education. These early immigrants wanted to know the ways of their new home.

After the Civil War, the Roman Catholic parents usually sent their children to the parochial schools. Among them were St. Patrick's in the heart of the city and St. James in the Ironbound section, where many people lived close to the factories in which they worked.

St. Vincent's Academy on West Market Street is operated by the Sisters of Charity of St. Elizabeth, the first congregation of religious women in New Jersey. Once the school served the city's Irish population, as did St. Joseph's Roman Catholic Church across the street. Today, the students are African American, Hispanic, and Portuguese. The aim remains the same, mixing technical training and liberal arts to prepare the high school students for the future world. The girls also must participate in a community service program to help the community in the Central Ward.

Essex Catholic High School occupied the handsome Mutual Benefit Insurance Company building at 298 Broadway from the time it was organized in 1958 until it moved to the former East Orange Catholic Girls High School at 125 Glenwood Avenue, East Orange, in 1980. In 1999, the school changed its name to the Bishop Francis Essex Catholic High School. The insurance company, meanwhile, moved to a new building at 520 Broad Street, opposite Washington Park; it is now a business called IDT. The Broadway building became the Broadway House For Continuing Care in 1997.

In 1814, Anna Richards, daughter of Reverend Dr. James Richards, organized the first Sunday school in the city for African Americans at the First Presbyterian Church. Besides the three "Rs," Miss Richards also instructed her students about the Presbyterian faith.

St. Vincent's Academy is a Catholic girls high school on West Market Street, opposite St. Joseph's Plaza.

These young students from the Beacon Street German American School pose for this 1885 class portrait.

In 1864, the Newark Board of Education requested James Baxter, an African American from Philadelphia, to come to Newark and start the Colored School of Newark on Market Street. Later, it was moved to State Street adjacent to the House of Prayer. Baxter was determined that his students would become excellent scholars. He was a strong disciplinarian in the school and he fought the school officials and the public to see that his pupils had the same advantages as other children. One of these fights was to have his graduates admitted to Newark High School—he was successful. These graduates included his own five children, who all went to college and on to professional careers. One daughter was the first African-American woman teacher in the city; another became a dentist. When he retired in 1909, the school was closed and African Americans then attended the city's various other schools.

St. Benedict's College was founded by Benedictine monks from Germany in Newark in 1868. The college, which ceased operation during World War I, also conducted a preparatory school that continues to exist. Built to teach German, Irish, and Italian youths, it now has a student body made up of Hispanic and African-American youths. Although the ethnic dynamics have changed, its aim is the same: to give its students the best college preparatory education that is possible. In 2000, the school added a dormitory for 60 students. In 2001, it is scheduled to add a kindergarten through eighth grade school for St. Mary's School on its 14-acre campus on Martin Luther King Boulevard at Springfield Avenue.

The New Jersey College of Pharmacy began in 1892, joined Rutgers in 1927, and became known as Rutgers College of Pharmacy, the first appearance of Rutgers College in Newark.

New York University reached across the Hudson River and the meadows to bring the arts to Newark in the Newark Institute of Arts and Sciences. Others followed, with the Mercer Beasley School of Law in 1926 and Dana College in 1930, sponsored by the New Jersey Law School just after the stock market crashed. Although the spirit was willing, the Seth Boyden School of Business was opened in 1929, but the money and credit were weak as the Depression heightened. Dana College absorbed both New Jersey Law School, which had started in 1908, and Seth Boyden School of Business in 1933. A year later, Mercer Beasley School of Law and Newark Institute of Arts and Sciences joined each other and opened as the University of Newark. Dana College and the University of Newark merged in 1935.

These different schools and programs all became part of Rutgers in 1946, when it opened night classes and a graduate school of banking. The school has expanded into Rutgers-Newark, with both day and evening classes. Its campus is between Washington Street and Martin Luther King Boulevard. The new law school building on Washington Street opened in 1999. After it became part of Rutgers, the law school moved into the American Insurance Company building, where it held classes for about 20 years. Rutgers University in Newark is built entirely on

The New Jersey College of Pharmacy, founded in 1892, became the first Newark facility taken over by Rutgers University in 1927.

The Paul Robeson Center at Rutgers University, Newark, is named for the multi-talented actor, singer, author, and athlete, who graduated from Somerville, New Jersey High School, and Rutgers College in New Brunswick.

urban renewal land, and like the four other colleges in the city, it continues to expand.

Like Princeton, Rutgers began as a theological school in 1766 to train ministers for the Dutch Reformed Church in New Brunswick. Its original name was Queens College, but it was changed when the Revolutionary War began and was named for Colonel Henry Rutgers, a philanthropist. In addition to the Newark and New Brunswick campuses, Rutgers has a campus in Camden. The New Jersey College for Women, started in 1918, joined Rutgers in 1955 and was renamed Douglass College.

The Seton Hall Law School opened in Newark in 1951. It is the only law school in New Jersey operated by a private university, which became a university in 1950. The college was formed by the Roman Catholic Archdiocese of Newark and it was named by Bishop James Roosevelt Bayley, first bishop of Newark, for his aunt, Sister Elizabeth Ann Seton, founder of the first American community of the Sisters of Charity. The university is located on a 58-acre campus in South Orange. The law school was located on Clinton Street, and the new high-rise law school on Mulberry Street at Market Street contains classrooms on the lower floors and offices that are leased on the upper floors.

Seton Hall University opened its College of Medicine and Dentistry in Jersey City in 1956. Later, the State took over the operation of the college and sought another location. An estate in Morris County was considered for the new college, but a site opposite the Newark City Hospital containing 50 acres was selected.

This selected area bounded by Bergen Street, Norfolk Street, South Orange Avenue, and Twelfth Avenue set off protests by 1,500 families occupying dwellings in the area.

Several opposition groups such as the Newark Area Planning Association and the Black Berets were formed. Multiple hearings were conducted. Promises were made to relocate the displaced families and tempers flared. The land was purchased, and temporary facilities were constructed for the opening of the school in 1969. It had been only a few months since the July 1967 riot had divided the city's population, and somehow, the 1,500 people were moved without major incident. Early in 1970, the work was able to begin on temporary buildings. The complex is still being expanded now as the university conducts community health service facilities for the neighborhood and community meetings in its auditorium. At first, the medical and dental departments were separate; now they are united in one university. The City Hospital was named Martland Hospital for Dr. Harrison Martland, who was noted for his work with radiation victims. The building was renamed University Hospital when the university was located across the street from it.

Newark College of Engineering became New Jersey Institute of Technology around 1975, when it expanded its curriculum to include architecture. The institution was founded in 1881 as the Newark Technical School and became Newark College of Engineering for day students in 1919, and Newark Tech at night. The school now covers 34 acres along Martin Luther King Boulevard. As a commuter college, it waited until 1979 to open its first dormitory on Bleeker Street for 230 students. The school also rented rooms at the YMWCA for its students until additional housing could be provided.

The Seton Hall University Law School was established in Jersey City by Seton Hall College. It later moved to a facility on Newark's Clinton Street. The new law school is now located on Mulberry and Market Streets.

Students are seen leaving the Newark High School of Fine and Industrial Arts at the close of the school day in 1987.

Essex County College was one of 19 community colleges opened by the State Department of Higher Education in 1966 to provide two-year associate degrees in the arts, science, and applied sciences. Most of its students hold full-time jobs and many are older than the traditional college student and plan to continue their education after graduation. In addition to the Newark campus, which has been expanded, the college conducts classes in West Caldwell.

The Rabbinical College of New Jersey was founded in 1956, and for a time was located in a one-family house on Grumman Avenue at Parkview Terrace. It moved to 226 Sussex Avenue in Morristown in the 1960s, where it has flourished. It is a branch of the world-wide Lublavitch Hasidic movement.

An insurance company building was converted into a makeshift school structure. The American Insurance Company skyscraper on Washington Park, built in the Georgian Revival style in 1929–1930, became the Rutgers University Samuel Newhouse Center for Law and Justice in 1970. It was used until 2000, when the law school moved to a new building on its main Newark campus on Washington Street.

In the fall of 2000, the board of education began alternative classes for youngsters who were failing their coursework. The Twilight Program is conducted from 3:30 to 7:30 p.m., Monday through Friday, in six area high schools. In the small Twilight classes, students advance to the next grade as soon as they master the skills of the grade they are taking. Four basic classes are given—math, social studies, language arts, and sciences—and students are required to take a high school proficiency test in the 11th grade. The teachers take special training to instruct in the program. School authorities believe the children are better motivated, attend classes more faithfully, and focus while they are in the classroom. Most of the children work a variety of local jobs before they come to school, and they also are expected to do volunteer work.

There are some 70 public, private, and parochial schools in Newark. There are 15 high schools, such as traditional schools like Barringer, Central, East Side, West Side, South Side (now Malcolm X Shabazz High School), and Weequahic, and also specialized institutions of instruction, like Newark High School of Fine and Industrial Arts, University High School, and Science High School, for students who qualify after examinations. In addition to the public and private schools, there are educational facilities to teach specialized curriculums besides the regular academic subjects to address the needs and culture of Newark's diverse population.

Education has always been important to the people of Newark. It has evolved to meet the needs of a changing population. For example, several Weequahic High School graduates from the 1960s have formed an alumni association to raise scholarship money for current graduates. When the prize-winning school band needed uniforms, anonymous donors supplied the estimated $75,000 money for them. In the public school systems, special schools have been established to help the talented student reach his/her full potential and to accommodate the needs of the disruptive and challenged student to achieve his/her potential. Others schools assist the child with handicaps or other problems. The five colleges offer a wide range of subjects and opportunities to students who attend their classes.

Pupils at West Side High School are seen exiting the school by the front entrance in 1982. Schools in Newark were initially named for their location in the city, such as East Side and South Side.

7. IN GOD WE TRUST

Each ethnic group that settled in Newark opened a church. By the nineteenth century, Newark was known as the "City of Churches." Newark's original settlers were second-generation colonists, and most of them were children of the first settlers in the Massachusetts or Connecticut colonies. The Newark settlement was soon augmented by a few Dutch, some Germans, Scotch, Scotch-Irish, English, and Irish settlers. While they may have come from different church backgrounds, the first church in Newark was the Congregational Church brought from the New Haven, Connecticut area by Reverend Abraham Pierson.

The church joined the Presbytery of Philadelphia about 1717, and most Presbyterian churches in Essex County are descendants of "Old First," as it was known. The original church was located across the street from the present edifice built in 1791. The second structure at the same site was burned during the Revolution when Reverend Dr. Alexander Macwhorter was pastor. Like most Presbyterian ministers of his time, he was an avid supporter of the Revolutionary cause, a fact that caused local people to call the Revolution, a Presbyterian War. This was the only church in town for 80 years.

The second church in Newark was started by a Presbyterian, Colonel Joshua Ogden, who cut his hay on a sunny Sunday after a week of rain in 1733. Censured by the Presbyterian Session, he left the church and spearheaded the founding of Trinity Cathedral in 1746, an Episcopal church. The original building, used as a hospital during the Revolutionary War, was badly damaged and a new sanctuary was built in 1809, incorporating parts of the old building and adding a steeple and a portico. It was designated a cathedral in 1917 and became St. Philip's-Trinity Cathedral in 1967, when St. Philip's, built in 1852, on Martin Luther King Boulevard was burned.

Newark's third denomination was the Baptist church, started in Lyons Farms on April 26, 1769, by 12 persons from the Scotch Plains Baptist Church, which in turn had started on September 6, 1747, by members of the Piscataway Baptist

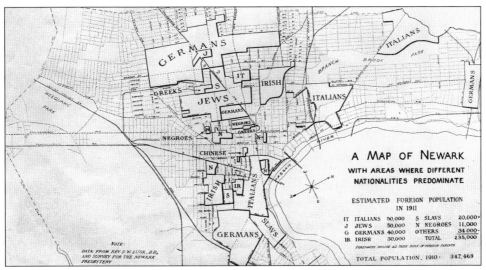

Reverend D.W. Lusk designed this 1911 map of Newark to show the areas "where different nationalities predominate."

Church, founded in 1707. The congregation met in members' homes until a small, white-frame church was erected on the Upper Road near Divident Hill. According to local legend, like Trinity, this church was also used for hospital purposes during the Revolutionary War.

The original building was replaced in 1874, and the present structure was built in 1908. A classroom building was added in 1971 by the Calvary Gospel Church, which had taken the church over. The Lyons Farms Baptist Church was renamed the Elizabeth Avenue Baptist Church about 1902, and it served as the mother church for all the Baptist churches in Newark and the First Baptist Church in Hillside. Reverend George McNeely served the church for 56 years. When he retired in 1964, the church was sold to the Calvary Gospel Church, an unaffiliated congregation. The new classroom building is used for its day school. The church was originally organized in the Central Ward. The old First Baptist Church, which once stood on Halsey Street at Academy Street, became the Peddie Memorial Baptist Church on Broad Street, when Mrs. T.B. Peddie, wife of the famous merchant, endowed it.

Located at 24 Mulberry Street, St. John's Roman Catholic Church, founded in 1826, has become the commuter's church, serving people enroute to the Penn Station for trains. It was the first Roman Catholic church in Newark and the first in the area. People from Elizabethtown walked across the meadows to attend it. It also has been known as the "people's church" because of its special services and concern for the poor. It conducts a daily lunch program for Newark's homeless outside the church fence.

Saint Patrick's Pro-Cathedral served as the Archdiocese of Newark's Cathedral from 1853 to 1956, when Sacred Heart became the cathedral. Located on

The Cathedral Basilica of the Sacred Heart, the fifth largest cathedral in the United States and the seat of the Diocese of Newark, is visible behind the cherry blossoms in Branch Brook Park.

Washington Street in the James Street Common Historic District, the Gothic Revival–styled building houses a variety of social programs for the central city. A recent grant for $350,981 from the New Jersey Historic Trust was used to eliminate water penetration to the building that threatened it and to restore the building's deteriorating exterior. Reverend James Roosevelt Bayley was the first head of the Newark Diocese.

The Fourth Presbyterian Church was started by African Americans who withdrew from "Old First" in May 1835 and established their own church on Plane Street, then on Washington Street, with the aid of Theodore Frelinghuysen. It later became known as the Central Presbyterian Church and for a time was opposite the Hiker's Statue on Clinton Avenue. After a fire, it was relocated to the vacant structure of the Second Presbyterian Church on Washington Street. In early records, a First African-American Presbyterian Church was also listed at 221 Plane Street, but it may have been the same congregation.

At one time, there were some 18 to 20 Presbyterian churches in Newark. One of these was the High Street Presbyterian Church on the hill above the initial settlement, where the well-to-do people lived. Designed by John Welch, a New Jersey architect, the church was built in 1850, in the English Gothic style using brownstone from the northern part of the city and including slate roofs and stained-glass windows. Carrere and Hastings, architects, drew the plans for an addition in 1890 for the Sunday school wing. The wing contains a 16-foot rose window believed to have been designed by Louis Comfort Tiffany, who had a factory in the city. The original French stained-glass windows in the sanctuary also were replaced by Tiffany windows.

The High Street Presbyterian Church merged with Old First Presbyterian Church in 1926, and the sanctuary was sold to St. James AME Church in 1944. In the 1990s, the church obtained a loan from the New Jersey Historic Trust for $1,250,000—the largest ever made by the trust for its restoration—and it was completed in 2000. A preparatory school has been erected adjacent to the church on Court Street for children of members. The 3,000-member congregation has an active roster of social service programs.

Only the facade of the South Park–Calvary United Presbyterian Church on Broad Street at Lincoln Park is still standing. Built in 1855 and designed by John Welch, the church was considered to be one of the best examples of the Greek Revival style in the area. The Ionic-columned portico and Greek towers still stand. The church was taken over by the Lighthouse Mission. Later, the structure was badly damaged in a fire. The mission was moved to a building nearby to continue its work, and all but the front of the building was removed. Flowers are planted in front of it each year.

Only the remnants of the old Wickliffe Presbyterian Church are left. It, too, is being preserved in the University Heights section as a monument to the century

A beautiful example of Greek Revival architecture, the South Park Presbyterian Church, dedicated on February 15, 1855, was designed by John Welch.

(1889 to 1989) that it stood on Thirteenth Avenue, and it was the oldest African-American Presbyterian congregation in the city. A plaque on its ruins relates its story. Other African-American churches on the eve of the Civil War included St. Philip's African Episcopal Church at 429 High Street, which has united with Trinity Episcopal Cathedral, and the First and Second African Methodist Churches.

Grace Episcopal Church at 950 Broad Street was organized in 1837. The present building, designed by John Upjohn, was completed in 1848 in the English perpendicular Gothic style. The 1850 House of Prayer, also Episcopalian, was designed by Frank Wills in the English Gothic style. The small brownstone church is similar to those village churches found in England.

The North Reformed Church at 510 Broad Street was built in 1857–1859, and once was the largest Reformed church in America, with a congregation of 1,800 members. The structure was refurbished after fires in 1922 and 1931. The Clinton Avenue Reformed Church was built at 27 Lincoln Park in 1868–1872 and has become Iglesia Pentecostal Roca de Salvacion (Rock of Salvation Pentecostal Church). Efforts are being made today to preserve it. The Trinity Reformed Church, at 483 Ferry Street, continues to function within the community.

St. Joseph's Roman Catholic Church on Lafayette Street was the first Catholic church in the area to serve the Spanish and Portuguese residents. Built in 1858, the church contained catacombs and crypts with wax likenesses of Spanish saints. St. James Roman Catholic Church on Lafayette and Jefferson Streets was dedicated in 1866 to serve the Ironbound's Irish population. The brownstone church had a 250-foot steeple completed in 1884. The structure was abandoned in the 1970s and razed for a parking lot for the St. James Hospital. Our Lady of

Both the church's influence and local English classes played important roles in the immigrant experience in Newark.

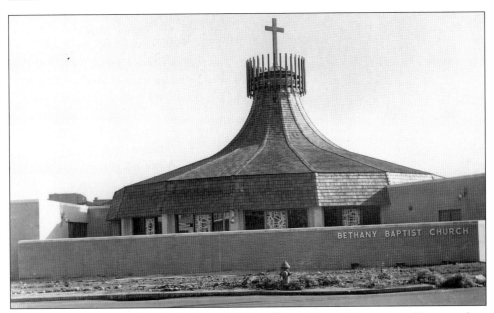

The Bethany Baptist Church, built in 1976 on West Market Street, resembles a modern version of an African hut.

Fatima Roman Catholic Church on Congress Street now serves the area, which has a large Portuguese population. The Ironbound's only synagogue, which never grew large enough to have its own spiritual leader, now is used as a day care center for Our Lady of Fatima Roman Catholic Church.

Another church devoted to the Irish immigrants was St. Joseph's Roman Catholic Church, dedicated in 1880. It was built opposite St. Vincent's Academy, a private school for Catholic girls, on West Market Street. After the Irish population moved to the suburbs, the Newark Archdiocese closed the parish in 1979. The church was purchased and redesigned as St. Joseph's Plaza by New Community Corporation (NCC). It was rededicated on April 18, 1985, to house the administrative offices of NCC. Architect Roz Li of New York City remodeled the building to contain a sandwich shop, the Priory Restaurant, the New Community Federal Credit Union, a spa and wellness center, and the United Hospitals Health care. Jazz concerts are featured in the former atrium each Thursday night. Offices on the second floor open off a balcony that circles the atrium. The offices are arranged so that the sunrays filtering through the stained-glass windows reflect on the rug in the atrium. The health club is situated in the basement. A glass-enclosed elevator carries people from floor to floor. NCC tenants also have urban gardens adjacent to their rental units.

The Bethany Baptist Church, organized in 1871 by an African-American congregation, dedicated its new sanctuary in 1976 on West Market Street. The architecture includes a mixture of African forms with Christian symbols. Its roofline, for instance, resembles a roofline on a traditional African building. A

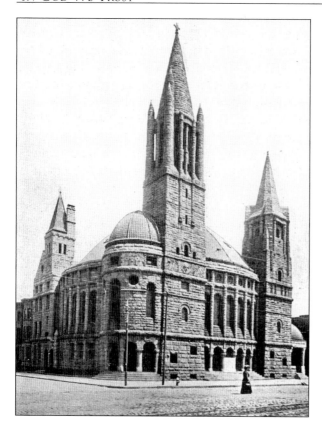

The First Baptist Peddie Memorial Church, located on Broad Street, was organized in 1801 and named as a result of an endowment from Mrs. Thomas Baldwin Peddie, his widow. Thomas Peddie, who served as Newark's mayor from 1866 to 1868, was a major manufacturer of trunks and traveling bags.

plaque has been placed on one of the townhouses on Society Hill to mark the church's original location.

Designed as a Victorian Gothic church by William A. Potter and built in 1874–1884, the Belleville Avenue Congregational Church became the Clinton Memorial African Methodist Episcopal Zion Church at 151 Broadway in 1930. The AME Zion church was founded in 1822 and it is the oldest African-American congregation in the city.

The First Baptist Peddie Memorial Church on Broad Street at Fulton Street is named for Thomas Baldwin Peddie, whose wife donated the money for it. Built in 1890, it replaced two earlier structures for the First Baptist Church, both small white buildings. An 80-foot-high dome rests above the sanctuary. The circular auditorium features rich paneling, some 200 doors, and 173 stained-glass windows.

Once, there were a dozen German-speaking congregations in Newark. They included three Presbyterian churches, one Evangelical Lutheran, one German Baptist, one Dutch Reformed, two Episcopal, two Roman Catholic, and two Methodists. Of these original German-speaking congregations, only St. Mary's Roman Catholic Church, now St. Mary's Abbey, appears to be functioning in Newark.

St. Lucy's Roman Catholic Church in the old First Ward was an Italian church, but the neighborhood moved away twice. At one time, it was surrounded by tenements, and these were removed for the Columbus Homes, a housing project, which has since been razed. Now, a large park-like area is being prepared in front of the church and two-story housing is replacing the apartments.

St. John's Ukrainian Catholic Church in the West Ward, built in 1962, serves the large Ukrainian population that has moved into the area. St. John's also supplies priests to Immaculate Conception Ukrainian Catholic Church in Hillside, where many of the Ukrainians also have moved farther out into the suburbs.

The oldest synagogue in Newark is still standing on Prince Street, once the home of Newark's Jewish population, and is ready for its third tenants. The synagogue was built by Oheb Shalom Congregation, which separated from Newark's first synagogue, B'nai Jeshurun. The congregation moved to a larger building on High Street and then to South Orange. The Metropolitan Baptist Church took the building over and used it until it built a new church. The Greater Newark Conservancy purchased the 116-year-old building and is restoring it for use by the conservancy. David Abramson, the architect, found that the Moorish Revival structure needed major work to repair vandalism after the Baptist church moved. The structure will be used as a research and education center. A plant nursery will be built beside it, and the grounds will be landscaped to Springfield Avenue.

St. Lucy's Roman Catholic Church was founded in 1891 for Newark's Italian population. This structure was built in 1925 and it contains a national shrine to St. Gerard Maiella.

115

Reverend James A. Aloupis (left), the pastor of St. Nicholas Greek Catholic Church, is seen here with Bishop Silas (second from left) of the Greek Orthodox Archdiocese of North and South America. They are honoring Mary and Michael Mastakas for their dedicated church and community service at ceremonies on December 9, 1973.

Movement of populations and shortages of priests have caused unification of some churches. Two of these are Blessed Sacrament Roman Catholic Church at 610 Clinton Avenue in the Clinton Hill section and St. Charles Borromeo Roman Catholic Church at 84 Custer Avenue in the Weequahic section. Blessed Sacrament was started in 1902, when some of the congregation from St. Leo's Roman Catholic Church in Irvington separated to start a new parish. The 3-acre Schwartz estate at Clinton Place and Millington Avenue was purchased in June 1903 for a new church. Mass was celebrated at the home of Frank Finley at 34 Homestead Park until a chapel was completed on November 26, 1903. The parish grew, and property was purchased on June 26, 1907, on Van Ness Place and Clinton Avenue. The first Mass in the new and present church was celebrated October 5, 1913. The church became famous for its band, the Golden Knights.

Property was purchased at Custer and Peshine Avenues for a new parish, St. Charles Borromeo, on July 21, 1909, as the subdivision of the Weequahic section was beginning. The church was spared when Route 78 was cut through, and the Weequahic Presbyterian Church nearby was demolished. The two Catholic churches merged in 1999 with Reverend Kenneth Jennings as the administrator. The mostly African-American congregation provides several community services, such as a food pantry, and several social activities, like the young adult liturgical dance ministry, the Gospel choir, and the Rosary and Holy Name Societies.

There is only one active Greek church, St. Nicholas Greek Orthodox Church, at 555 Martin Luther King Boulevard, six Kingdom Halls for the Jehovah's Witnesses, two United Churches of Christ (Congregational), three mosques, and many Apostolic, Assembly of God, Pentecostal, and Fellowship churches.

St. Casimir's Roman Catholic Church was built on Pulaski Street in 1920 for the Polish community. A fire a few years ago threatened the church, but it has been restored to its original beauty. One of its features is the Black Madonna. The historic church is listed on both the state and national historic registers.

In many instances, as in the case of the Pilgrim Church of New Jersey in the former Newark YM-YWHA, the Wells Cathedral of God in Christ Tabernacle in the former Oheb Shalom's sanctuary, or the Hopewell Baptist Church in the former sanctuary of B'nai Jeshurun, all on Martin Luther King Boulevard, efforts have been made to preserve and improve the architectural beauty of the church. An addition at the former First Congregational Church on Clinton Avenue

Temple B'nai Jeshurun, the oldest congregation in Newark, was formed in 1847 at 338 Washington Street. This beautiful structure on High Street became the congregation's final home in Newark in 1916. The temple moved to South Orange Avenue in South Orange in 1973.

St. Barnabas Episcopal Church on West Market Street at Sussex Avenue is a typical small Anglican country church. Built in 1864, this church is listed as a historic site.

became a Greek Orthodox Church, and now a Baptist church has planted a small flower garden in front of it. Spanish, Portuguese, French, and Arabic are spoken in congregations for Hispanic Americans, Portuguese or Brazilians, Haitians, Arabs or Indians from India. Each group that has arrived has shown its faith in God in its own way.

Religion in Newark today has changed. The worshippers no longer sit quietly with their hands folded and their heads bowed. Chances are they may be standing, clapping their hands, and moving around. Most Newarkers, however, express a belief in God, and in comparison to the first Puritan Newarkers, this devotion is expressed in a more joyful manner. In most cases, the people appreciate the old sanctuaries built years ago. Many of them have been lovingly restored to their former glory, except for the removal or addition of different symbols. Because attendance is no longer compulsory, the sanctuaries have smaller participants in their services, but the belief in a higher being is alive and well.

8. At One's Leisure

Newark has two concert halls: the Newark Symphony Hall (the former Mosque Theater) and the New Jersey Performing Arts Center. The Mosque was opened in 1925 by the Salaam Temple, and it features a 3,500-seat auditorium. The hall was operated first by the temple for mass meetings, lectures, and concerts. In the 1930s, Mrs. Parker O. Griffith, wife of the owner of the Griffith Piano Company, brought opera companies, major orchestras, and musicians to the hall. In 1965, it was leased by the City and the name was changed to the Newark Symphony Hall for the New Jersey Symphony Orchestra, which made the place its base of operations. Other rooms in the building became rehearsal halls, studios, and offices for other related musical groups, while a huge banquet hall was operated in the basement.

The home of Dr. William Burnet, a Revolutionary War medical doctor, once stood on the site of the Newark Symphony Hall. His son, David G. Burnet, was an early political leader of Texas, when it was formed as a separate republic.

The New Jersey Performing Arts Center on Park Place contains two theaters: the Prudential Hall, where major concerts are presented, and the Victoria Hall, for plays and smaller musical groups. In October 1997, it became the home for the New Jersey Symphony Orchestra and attracts major musicians and audiences from across New York and New Jersey.

The New Jersey Symphony Orchestra has six other venues in which it appears; these include the Community Theater in Morristown; the War Memorial in Trenton; the John Harms Center for the Arts, Englewood; the State Theater, New Brunswick; the Count Basie Theater in Red Bank; and Princeton University. In addition, the orchestra or soloists, duets, trios, quartets, or ensembles have appeared in more than 170 churches, schools, and parks throughout the state. They also have played in New York City, Philadelphia, Dublin, and the Adare Festival in Ireland, Washington, D.C., Wolf Trap Farm Park in Vienna, Virginia, Long Island, and in Connecticut.

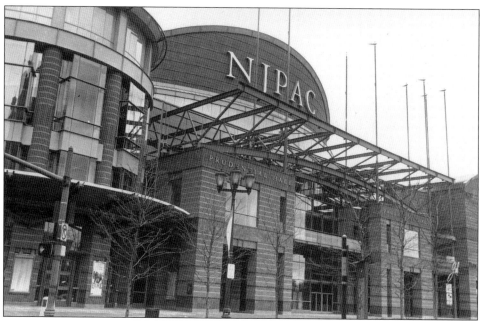

This is the entrance to the New Jersey Performing Arts Center (NJPAC), which opened in Newark in October 1997.

The orchestra is an outgrowth of the unification of several groups in Newark and surrounding areas who loved music and loved to play. The first of these was the Mannergesangverein (Men's Choral Society), formed by the Germans in Newark in 1846. It became the Eintracht (Harmony) Society and participated in many competitions with other singing groups after 1872. In 1914, the group changed its name to the Newark Symphony Orchestra because of the intense hatred of all things German during World War I. The Haydn Orchestra of Orange was organized in Orange in 1889. The Newark Symphony Orchestra (NJSO) and the Haydn Orchestra of Orange joined each other in the 1920s.

Another musical group, the Llewellyn Ensemble began playing chamber music in 1917, and the Montclair Orchestra was formed in 1920. The Llewellyn was invited to play for the first time at the Montclair Art Museum on November 17, 1922, recognized as the official date of the founding of NJSO. The Llewellyn Ensemble and the Montclair Orchestra decided to pool their money and hire Philip James as their conductor. When the group played in Montclair, it was called the Montclair Orchestra; when it appeared in Orange, it was called the Symphony Society of the Oranges and Maplewood. In order to end the confusion, the name was changed to the New Jersey Orchestra. It was composed only of string instruments, augmented occasionally by paid musicians from the New York Philharmonic Orchestra.

When the Haydn Orchestra of Orange joined the ensemble in the 1928–1929 season with its brass instruments, the orchestra had both brass and string instruments on a permanent basis for the first time. By the mid-1930s, the name was changed again and the word "Symphony" was inserted, making it the New Jersey Symphony Orchestra, and it has used that name ever since.

At first, only three concerts were planned annually, and except for some world-famous soloists, the members went unpaid. Gradually, the number of concerts and the scope of the music played expanded. Today, there are a series of concerts by Mozart, Wagner, Beethoven, and other great composers each year. Replacement of the volunteer orchestra members began in 1955, when only professional, paid musicians could appear at the tenth anniversary concert to celebrate the founding of the United Nations at the Mosque Theater.

By the time Henry Lewis became the first African American to become the director of a major symphony orchestra in 1968, all the orchestra members were professional and paid. The orchestra now has about 75 members. Up to 60 percent of the members have been women. The orchestra was homeless until 1965, when it moved into the Mosque Theater, and the theater became Newark Symphony Hall.

The orchestra presents young people's concerts and open dress rehearsals. Since 1976, it has conducted annual Young Artists Auditions and the winners are invited to play with the orchestra in at least one concert. Nadja Salerno-Sonnenberg, a violinist, who was one of the winners in 1976, has become internationally famous in the music world. Richard Kogan, a pianist and a winner that same year, became a physician and occasionally appears in concerts. NJSO has developed a master teacher collaborative with resource books for use prior to children attending concerts. A grant from the Geraldine R. Dodge Foundation pays for the course, which offers graduate credits at Seton Hall University in South Orange.

Since its inception, the orchestra has had a dozen musical directors and nine executive directors. Rene Pollain followed Philip James in 1929. Pollain hired professional musicians for some concerts. He returned to his home in France when World War II began in 1939 and disappeared in 1940. Dr. Frieder Weissman became the third director, serving from 1940 to 1947. Samuel Antek, the fourth musical director, introduced children's and pops concerts.

The orchestra made its debut on Radio Station WNJR on January 26, 1948. Dr. Edna McEachem of Montclair State Teachers College gave previews of the major works to be played at three concerts. Dr. Antek also formed the Friends of the New Jersey Symphony Orchestra and the Junior New Jersey Symphony for students and joined the Papermill Playhouse in the first New Jersey Summer Music Festival at the playhouse in 1956. He suffered a heart attack and died in January 1958

The fifth director was Matyas Abas in 1958, who increased the children's concerts and the length of the concert season. Quartets were organized to play at schools and Women's Committees in Maplewood/South Orange and Livingston and local committees were organized to conduct fund-raising for the orchestra. The Newark Boys' Chorus grew out of a boys' chorus organized by Kenneth

Henry Lewis became the first African-American director of a major orchestra when he was appointed by the New Jersey Symphony Orchestra. He is seen here with his wife, Marilyn Horne, who performed as an opera singer.

Schermerhorn, the sixth conductor. The Duke and Duchess of Windsor were guests at a Symphony Ball that he organized. The NJSO began appearing on WNJU-TV (Channel 47), expanded its concert season, and formed a junior symphony and a symphony chorus.

Henry Lewis took music to the streets of Newark in the riot-torn area when he became director in 1968. He believed that people in the poorest neighborhoods could learn to love and understand classical music. His wife, Marilyn Horne, was frequently the soloist at his concerts. He had the men in the orchestra wear tails instead of the traditional tuxedo. One night, however, he appeared at a concert in shirtsleeves. He explained that he had left his car parked on Broad Street during the pre-concert rehearsal and that the suit he planned to wear was stolen. He had come as he was. His daughter, Angela, donated a grant in her father's name to the orchestra for the training of young musicians.

Max Rudolf, director in 1976–1977, is credited with developing a three-year master plan and signing a two-year contract with the musicians' union, expanding the concert series, and introducing special features such as the *Messiah*. Thomas Michalak's directing of Sarah Vaughan, a Newarker, in March 1980, in a Gershwin concert called *Rhapsody in Blue* won Vaughan an Emmy on PBS television. George Manahan, associate conductor, took over when Michalak failed to appear one night and continued to direct until 1985, when Hugh Wolff was named director.

Wolff observed that "when people think of New Jersey, they think of Bruce Springsteen and Frank Sinatra. The time has come to add the New Jersey

Symphony Orchestra to the top of the list." He inaugurated a chamber orchestra series and he mixed pop and classical concerts together. During his tenure, the orchestra participated twice in the Adare Festivals at County Limerick, Ireland, and appeared eight times at Carnegie Hall. He resigned in August 1992 to become director of the St. Paul Chamber Orchestra.

Zdenek Macal was appointed the director on June 2, 1992. He is the first native of Czechoslovakia to serve as the director. While he was director, the orchestra moved from the Newark Symphony Hall to the New Jersey Performing Arts Center (NJPAC) in October 1997. Governor Thomas H. Kean announced plans for the center in 1989. Macal informed Lawrence Tamburri, executive director of the orchestra, that he will retire in June 2002, but will remain on staff for two additional years. Since its opening, the NJPAC has received raves for its acoustics. The building contains two restaurants and a gift shop. Its opening is reviving interest in other buildings around Military Park.

Several other sections of Newark are experiencing a renaissance of sorts. The Robert Treat Hotel has installed a new restaurant and several others have opened. Bears and Eagles Riverfront Stadium has opened for minor league baseball and a major stadium is planned, as are more restaurants, residences, and shops. Park areas are being extended along the Passaic River.

The Newark Boys' Chorus separated from the orchestra in 1978 and organized its own school near Newark Symphony Hall. The boys are instructed in music as well as the traditional curriculum. The chorus has appeared throughout the United States and has visited several foreign countries, including South Africa.

The Garden State Ballet, organized in 1959 by Fred Daniele at Newark Symphony Hall, was moved to Fairleigh Dickinson University in Rutherford in the mid-1980s.

The New Jersey Historical Society was organized in Trenton in 1845 and moved to Newark the following year. A Georgian Colonial limestone building was erected for the society in 1931 at 230 Broadway. The society moved to the former Essex Club building on Park Place on June 12, 1997. The Essex Club, once a political and corporate powerhouse, was organized in 1876. The five-story building was erected in 1926 by Guilbert and Betelle. The club disbanded in 1992. The New Jersey Historical Society obtained the building in April 1993, and Ford Farewell Mills were in charge of the alterations. The New Jersey Historical Society features timely exhibits, presents programs on local history, and conducts walking tours of the center city illustrating its social history. The society has a large assortment of books on New Jersey and information on genealogy.

The Newark Library Association was founded as a private institution in 1845. Before that, Reverend Abraham Pierson had 440 books in his individual library, which he apparently shared with some of the congregation, and in 1783, students at the Institutio Legalis of Newark were pooling books. Samuel Conger opened an Apprentices' Library for 700 apprentices in Newark on Saturday evenings— hardly the time that a youth would want to go to a library! Pressure from the community caused the formation of the private association. Shares of stock were

The Newark Public Library opened in 1901 at 5 Washington Street.

sold to raise money to purchase the books. The investors were assured of free admission, and all others were charged $2 a year.

It became the Newark Public Library in 1888, when it leased the former Park Theater on West Park Street for a library. Frank Hill, the librarian, supervised the construction of the present building at 5 Washington Street. Both Hill and John Cotton Dana, who followed him, were innovative and did everything they could to make books available to the people of Newark and to induce people to patronize the library. Hill introduced open shelves and children's books loaned to the city schools. Dana introduced foreign language books for the immigrants, donated business books and titles on art history and civic responsibility, distributed reading lists, and founded the Newark Museum on the top floor of the library. Dana's work was well known, and several students of library science came to study under him before working for libraries in other cities.

The library building at 5 Washington Street was erected in 1901 and has had several additions. A bronze high relief installed in 1909 is on the facade of the building, and Newark native John Flanagan created this art piece, entitled *Wisdom Instructing the Children of Men*. The library features a marble staircase, a central court, with murals representing knowledge. A decorative glass ceiling is above the court on the fourth floor. Exhibit cases on the second and third floors contain photographs, posters, rare books, and manuscripts mostly dealing with various facets of the city's history. Rooms are set aside for children, computers, the New

Jersey section, African-American and Hispanic culture and history, literacy programs, and general research. Every year when the federal income tax is due, authorities are available at the library to help in the preparation of the returns. Also, each month has a theme for a variety of concerts or lectures. A small auditorium on the fourth floor offers programs or motion pictures nearly every Saturday for children and adults.

The library also maintains 11 branches in each section of the city; they are listed as follows: Branch Brook at 235 Clifton Avenue; Clinton at 739 Bergen Street; First Avenue; Madison area at 790 Clinton Avenue; Mount Vernon School; North End at 722 Summer Avenue; Roseville at 99 Fifth Street; Springfield at 50 Hayes Street; Vailsburg at 75 Alexander Street; Van Buren at 140 Van Buren Street; and Weequahic at 355 Osborne Terrace. Each offers children and adult books and programs to meet the needs and interests of that particular neighborhood, including foreign language texts and public service opportunities such as blood pressure screening, sponsored by the Interfaith Health Services. Each of the branches has undergone extensive remodeling in recent years. At the Weequahic Branch, for instance, the second-floor children's room now serves as a community room for day care centers and local groups. The branch has seven public access computers and a Club Success homework program with two additional programs and two literary groups. The main library is scheduled for remodeling in 2002 and will include public parking, a restaurant, gift shop and library store, research carrels, air-conditioning of the entire structure, and accessibility to the stacks.

The museum moved into the new building at 49 Washington Street in 1926. Michael Graves, a Princeton architect, redesigned the building to incorporate the old Newark YWCA building and the Ballantine House into its complex. The pool in the Y has become the auditorium, while the old building contains the children's

Located on Washington Street, the Newark Museum (left) is pictured next to the historic residence of John Ballantine, now part of the museum.

The dining room of the John Ballantine Mansion featured a white linen tablecloth, French porcelain dishes, Hawkes cut stemware, and sterling silver flatware.

museum and museum offices. The central court houses a cafe. Access to an addition at the rear has been improved and turned into gallery areas.

The Ballantine House was designed by George Edward Harney, AIA (1840–1924) for John Holme Ballantine (1824–1895), son of Peter Ballantine (1791–1883), founder of the Ballantine Brewery in Newark in 1848. The residence was built in 1883–1885 of Philadelphia-pressed red brick and grey Wyoming sandstone and contains 17 rooms. The architecture is a blend of the Renaissance and Romanesque Revival styles. Carved floral and foliate designs decorate the top of the porch and front bay window, and carved Corinthian capitals top the grey granite porch columns. It is furnished with period pieces and at Christmas features Victorian decorations.

The walled garden at the rear contains the 1784 stone schoolhouse, moved from its original site at Elizabeth and Chancellor Avenues, a Fire Museum, located in the old carriage house, and a fountain from the old Prudential Insurance Company building on Broad Street. The Newark Fire Department Historical Association began holding annual musters and parades in 1977. All departments in the state are invited to enter their oldest equipment into the museum's collection.

The museum features a unique Tibetan exhibit. There also are many exhibits of Americana, including paintings, sculpture, jewelry, china, furniture, as well as European craftsmanship. A planetarium features regular shows, and the museum presents lectures in its auditorium on its exhibits, walking tours of the museum, and concerts in the garden and sponsors daytime tours of Newark, New Jersey, or nearby states, as well as tours to other countries.

Newark today has some 754 acres in parks, ball diamonds, playgrounds, tennis courts, football/soccer fields, and lakes. When Newark was settled, the early citizens designated the Upper Green to be the market place, which became Washington Park, and the Lower Green to be the parade ground, which became Military Park. Troops trained there for combat until after the Civil War. These early settlers set aside land to create South Park, so named in 1850. After the Civil War, the park's name was changed to honor the Great Emancipator: Lincoln.

The New Jersey State Legislature authorized the formation of the Essex County Park Commission in 1895. The first park created by the new commission was Branch Brook Park along the Belleville-line in the former Blue Jay Swamp. Originally, John Bogart and Nathan F. Barrett were hired to design the park, the first and largest county park in the nation in a city. In 1900, the firm of Frederick Law Olmsted was hired to revise and complete the plans for the 359.72-acre park. It was the first of seven Olmsted parks in Newark. The 4-mile-long park is about a quarter of a mile wide. A portion of the Morris Canal ran along its westerly side.

One of the many highlights of the Newark Museum is the Tibetan altar. Tibetans, such as these pictured at the altar, frequently visit the museum to inspect the exhibit of a disappearing culture.

The Ballantine Gate into Branch Brook Park, designed by Frederick Law Olmsted, welcomes people to the first Essex County park.

The Old Bloomfield Road is situated on the easterly side with Newark's oldest standing house—Sydenham House, built about 1710. The park included the reservoir, which once supplied fresh water to a private association of Newark residents. Special features besides the winding road, paths, and bridges are the Ballantine Gate, donated by Robert Ballantine in 1898, and more than 2,000 cherry trees donated by Louis Bamberger and his sister, Mrs. Felix Fuld, in 1927. The blossoms, more colorful than those in Washington, D.C., attract thousands of visitors every April.

Weequahic Park on the Hillside-Newark line with 311.33 acres is the second largest developed county park and was also designed by the Olmsted firm. It contains an 80-acre lake and an 18-hole golf course, as well as Divident Hill and a statue of Franklin Murphy, first president of the park commission and a former governor. U.S. Route 22 and the tracks for the Lehigh Valley Railroad, now part of New Jersey Transit, cut through the park.

Newark's other Frederick Law Olmsted–designed parks are West Side Park in the Central Ward, covering 31.36 acres and containing a community center with a gymnasium and a bandstand; Independence Park, covering 12.69 acres adjacent to East Side High School in the Ironbound or Down Neck section with a gazebo, bandstand, a senior citizen and playground field house, a lighted boccie court, and various other athletic courts; and Riverbank Park, along the Passaic River in the Ironbound section, covering 10.77 acres and featuring tennis and basketball courts.

The two remaining Olmsted-designed parks are Ivy Hill Park on Mount Vernon Place on the South Orange border and Vailsburg Park, adjacent to the Garden State Parkway in the Vailsburg section. The Ivy Hill Park covers 18.96 acres and was developed in 1938 for residents of Maplewood, Newark, South Orange, and Irvington. One acre of land containing six tennis courts abuts Seton Hall University in South Orange, and the university is permitted to use the courts without charge. There also are courts for basketball, three baseball fields, a combined football/soccer field, band concert area, and playground. The Vailsburg Park completed in the late 1920s was used by the United States Army in World Wars I and II for training, embarking, and recruiting, and again in 1952, when an anti-aircraft gun site was placed on a small portion until 1960. United Vailsburg Services schedules ball games and other activities in the park.

Mother Cabrini Park, named for Saint Frances Xavier Cabrini, the first American citizen to be canonized in the Roman Catholic Church, is situated on Market Street east of the Pennsylvania Station. The community organization Mother Cabrini Post 156, Catholic War Veterans commissioned artist Francesco Miozzo to produce the statue of Mother Cabrini, which was placed in the park in 1958. One of the schools organized by Mother Cabrini was once located on the site. The famed spiritual leader was known for establishing orphanages, hospitals, and day care centers. A bust of Jose Marti, liberator of Cuba, is located nearby in the park.

The Waverly Fair Grounds featured horse racing for about 50 years, from just after the Civil War until the early 1900s. Some of the fairgrounds area became Weequahic Park. The races were moved to Johnson Park in Piscataway.

Three boys fish in a pond at Branch Brook Park using boards from a nearby building site for rafts.

Close to Mother Cabrini Park is Peter Francisco Park, named for Peter Francisco, a Portuguese patriot who fought for the new nation in the American Revolution. Another tiny park on Broad Street, near St. Phillip's–Trinity Cathedral, is Monsignor Doane Park on Rector Street and Broad Street, featuring his statue by W. Clark Noble. Monsignor George Hobart Doane was an Episcopal priest who then became a Roman Catholic priest and pastor of St. Patrick's Roman Catholic Church. Doane was a chaplain in the Civil War and advocated opportunities in music and art, city planning, cleaner streets, efficient sewage, playgrounds, and shade trees in Newark.

The largest park in the Ironbound section, Independence Park, originally East Side Park, covers 12.5 acres between Adams and Van Buren Streets and Walnut and Oliver Streets. The park's name was changed on July 4, 1923, at the request of the residents. In 1987, a small park in the Central Ward at West Market Street and Twelfth Avenue, known as Wallace Park, was renamed William M. Ashby/Wallace Park for Ashby on his 97th birthday. Ashby was considered to be the dean of Newark's African-American community leaders. He established the Newark office of the Urban League in 1917 and helped to found the Newark Preservation and Landmarks Committee in 1973, and was a member of its board of trustees. The committee published his memoirs, *Tales Without Hate*, in 1980.

The board of commissioners of the City of Newark adopted a resolution on June 13, 1942, designating Milford Park, bounded by Elizabeth Avenue, Bigelow

Street, and Milford Avenue, as Schleifer Memorial Park to commemorate the death of Private Louis Schleifer, the first Newarker killed on December 7, 1941, at Pearl Harbor during the Japanese attack. Private Schleifer, a graduate of South Side High School in 1939, now Malcolm X Shabazz High School, served with the Fifth Bombardment Group of the Army Air Corps. He is said to have been observed running down the runway shooting a rifle at the enemy planes before he was killed.

The Jewish War Veterans of the United States erected a fountain and a flag pole in the center of the park. The words under an eagle on the monument state, "Dedicated to Those Who Sacrificed All to Preserve the Freedom and Equality of All." Unfortunately, the monument was vandalized. A portion of the monument was moved to the Rosenthal Garden in Temple Beth Shalom on Mount Pleasant Avenue in West Orange, where it was rededicated by the Pearl Harbor Survivors' Club of New Jersey on November 11, 1984. A poem by Private Schleifer is featured on the base of the restored monument.

A park was dedicated to the memory of Archie Callahan, a 19-year-old African-American mess attendant on the USS *Oklahoma* at Pearl Harbor. The Guyton-Callahan Post 152, American Legion, which met on Elizabeth Avenue, was also named in his honor. Kerrigan Boulevard in Vailsburg was named for Raymond Kerrigan, a machinist's mate on the USS *Vestal*, and Runiak Avenue on the Newark-Elizabeth city line, adjacent to Mount Olivet Cemetery, was named for Nicholas Runiak, a seaman on the USS *Arizona*. Sometime after these four men were honored, the City discovered that Eugene Eberhardt, another serviceman, also had been killed that day.

The pedestal on which the *Hiker*, a bronze statue of a Spanish-American soldier once stood, stands empty at McKinley Circle on Clinton Avenue at Irvine Turner Boulevard (Belmont Avenue). It was stolen in 1980. The statue by Allen G. Newman was unveiled on Memorial Day, 1914, as a gift to the City from the United Spanish War Veterans.

The Newark Schools Stadium, built in the 1920s on Bloomfield Avenue, usually featured two football games instead of the traditional one each Saturday during the season. High school graduations and summer concerts also took place in it. The William Untermann Stadium, adjacent to the Chancellor Avenue School, is used by Weequahic High School students both for practice and games. The high school also uses it for graduation ceremonies, and youths desiring to jog utilize the running track around it. The stadium is named for William Untermann, a municipal judge. The Newark Bears Stadium, named Ruppert Stadium, in the Ironbound section was used for games prior to World War II. After World War II, it was used for stock car races. It eventually fell into disuse and was razed. The Bears and Eagles Riverfront Stadium was built on Bridge Street close to the Newark Library for the minor league team. Another stadium near the Four Corners for the New Jersey Nets and Devils may be constructed shortly. The Four Corners (at Broad and Market Streets) have been designated as a historic district by the New Jersey Historic Trust.

The New Jersey Symphony Orchestra is seen here tuning up in the early 1990s.

WBG/Newark Public Radio 88 F.M. is Newark's 24-hour jazz station, which conducts a special Jazz Week each year. Started in 1979, the station is now located in a studio on Park Place near New Jersey PAC. The station's audience totals about 325,000 persons, with 15,000 members. It began broadcasting over the Internet in 1998, and it has picked up thousands more listeners. Its music includes full concerts, as well as gospel, blues, and Latin solos. The station also features programs from the Priory in Newark, the former St. Joseph's Roman Catholic Church, now the headquarters for New Community Corporation, some interviews with musicians, and news about jazz.

African-American and white musicians in Newark were known for their ability to play jazz in the city in the 1920s through the 1940s. Barbara Kukla, editor of the "Newark This Week Section" of the *Star Ledger* calls Newark "Swing City." In her book *Swing City 1925–1950* (Temple University Press, Philadelphia), Kukla notes that speakeasies were everywhere during Prohibition, especially in the black community. These "underground" bars provided music, dancing, and liquor at low cost. When the repeal of Prohibition came, the dance halls grew larger, but the cost for a drink remained low and there were few cover charges.

Until 1999, Newark held the Jazz Festival for a decade, and it was discontinued only when when Alex Boyd, Newark library director and chairman of the festival, became ill. There also is a Jazz Center at Rutgers-Newark. Jazz concerts are featured at Newark's two symphony halls: New Jersey PAC and the Newark Symphony Hall. The Newark Museum's lunchtime summer program in the garden and evening programs also feature jazz ensembles.

Newark jazz musicians include Sarah Vaughan, singer; Woody Shaw, trumpeter; Wayne Shorter, tenor saxophonist and composer; Andy Bey, singer;

Babs Gonzales (Lee Brown); Betty Carter, vocalist and band leader; Vinnie Burke (Vincenzo Bucci), band leader; (Walter) Gil Fuller, pianist-composer; Bobby Plater, alto saxophonist; Ike Quebec, tenor saxophonist; Larry Young, organist; Willie "the Lion" Smith, pianist; Carrie Smith, soloist; and Marlene Ver Planck.

Other stations in Newark include WNET, Channel 13 TV Public Television, Newark area; WHSE, Channel 68 TV at 390 West Market Street; WNEW TV Metromedia at 972 Broad Street; New Jersey Network at 50 Park Place; WNJR Radio Station at 1 Riverfront Plaza or 2 Park Place; and WNCE Radio Station at 323 Martin Luther King Boulevard.

Newarkers loved the theater. Theaters made their appearance just before the Civil War. Some of the early theaters included Library Hall, Atlantic Garden, Fox's Comique, Waldmann's, and Miner's Theater on Market Street (opened in 1886 on the future site of Paramount). The residents loved to see the try-outs of shows before they moved to Broadway.

Until the Depression wiped it out, the locals especially enjoyed live theater, serious plays, or variety shows. Among the stages kept busy were the Newark Opera House and the Empire, later featuring burlesque, both on Washington Street, and other theaters like the Broad on Broad Street (opposite the Newark Public Library), the Paramount, Loew's, Proctor's, Branford, the Shubert, and Adams. The passion for theater was so great among Newarkers that school truant officers would circulate through the audiences looking for children who had cut classes to attend a performance. Laurel Garden, which was usually used for boxing matches, sometimes featured shows.

The owners and builders of theaters called them palaces. The Empire Theater, later a burlesque house, started life as a legitimate theater featuring stage plays. In the early part of the twentieth century, Newark was a place for tryouts of new Broadway shows.

When silent motion pictures were shown in the 1920s, the program usually included a vaudeville act. Gradually, however, as double features, coming attractions, promotions, shorts, cartoons, the *March of Time*, and an episode of a continuous film were added to the programs, vaudeville disappeared. The New Theater opposite Washington Park continues to feature foreign language films as it did in the 1940s.

Featured in many early motion pictures, the Ritz Brothers—Harry, Al, and Jimmy—were products of Newark. Other actors whose roots were in Newark were John Amos, another comedian; Vivian Blaine, a singer and actress; Nick Massi, one of the Four Seasons; Paul Simon, singer and songwriter; Ruth St. Denis, dancer and choreographer; Gloria Gaynor, singer; Frankie Valli, singer; and Jack Warden, actor. Movies opened at first-run houses in New York City, then moved to the Branford, Loew's, Proctor's, or the Paramount before going to neighborhood theaters. Each motion picture would show for several weeks, so if it were missed in one place, the determined viewer could catch it somewhere else, usually nearby. Newark had nearly 40 neighborhood theaters.

The old Weequahic theater on Bergen Street became the Park and then a church. The Cameo on Elizabeth Avenue became a Baptist church. The Stanley Theater at 985 South Orange Avenue in the Vailsburg section was designed by Frank Grad, a popular architect, and opened in 1927. In 1968, it was purchased by the Father Vincent Monella Center of Italian Culture and became Casa Italiana. Like these other venues, it too changed from a theater to a house of worship.

Two theaters have been constructed since motion picture houses decided to show several features in smaller auditoriums at one time. One multiplex is in the Ironbound section, while the second is just above the University of Medicine and Dentistry. Both have fenced parking lots, which would be difficult to place adjacent to many of the older theaters.

The Newark team of the International Baseball League poses for a photograph in April 1925. Recently, Yogi Berra, who spearheaded the construction of the Bears and Eagles Stadium, has brought the much-loved sport back to the city with the Newark Bears, a minor league team.

Seen here c. 1920s, Loew's State Theater on Broad Street, near Hahne's Department Store, was showing the Trail of the Lonesome Pine. *The man on stilts was advertising the Palisades Park.*

Newark has had several outstanding athletes. For example, Weequahic High School has produced two athletes of note: Seymour "Swede" Masin, who excelled in all sports, and Alvin Attles (Class of 1955), a basketball player who became the coach of the Golden State Warriors and is currently the organization's vice president and assistant general manager. Rick Cerone, a professional baseball player, and Drew Pearson, a professional football player, were born in Newark. Of most recent fame, Shaquille O'Neal, a basketball player with the Los Angeles Lakers, is a product of Newark.

Mary Mapes Dodge, who lived with her father, James J. Mapes, at his farm, wrote *Hans Brinker, or the Silver Skates* in response to a plea from her two young sons to write a story about ice skating, which they loved. Years later, one of the sons visited Holland and asked for a book about Dutch life. He was handed his mother's book as the best one! Mrs. Dodge was editor of *St. Nicholas Magazine*, so named because she believed St. Nicholas always made children happy.

William Herbert, who used the name Frank Forrester, wrote hunting, fishing, and sporting books at his home, the "Cedars," near the Passaic River on the site of Mount Pleasant Cemetery. Albert Payson Terhune was noted for his stories about dogs. Dr. Thomas Dunn English created the "Ben Bolt" books, and Edward Stratemeyer created the following popular children's series of books: "Tom Swift," "Hardy Boys," "Nancy Drew," and the "Bobbsey Twins." Howard Garis, who created "Uncle Wiggily," the most famous rabbit of his time, wrote more than 12,000 stories about this enchanting character. Many of these stories appeared in the *Evening News* and were favorite bedtime stories for children.

The Lavradeiras do Minho, Portuguese dancers of Newark, perform the closing celebration of the Ethnic Week in Newark's Ironbound section in April 1979.

Mrs. E.C. Kinney, wife of William B. Kinney, editor of the *Daily Advertiser*, and Reverend Dr. Lyman Whitney Allen, pastor of the South Park Presbyterian Church, were both respected poets. Antoinette Scudder, a member of the family that owned the *Newark Evening News*, wrote the play the *Second Generation* and helped found the Papermill Playhouse in Millburn in the 1930s.

Newark has something for everyone's tastes and pleasures. Crowds flock to Branch Brook Park to see the cherry blossoms and to concerts at St. Joseph's Plaza, the Sacred Heart Basilica, the Museum Garden, NJPAC, or Newark Symphony Hall. Art may be viewed in the museum, the Newark Public Library, the City Without Walls, an assortment of galleries, or at special shows at sites like St. John's Roman Catholic Church. The five colleges offer lectures and other programs open to the public, many free of charge. The museum, Newark Preservation and Landmarks Committee, and the New Jersey Historical Society feature walking tours of various sections of the city. Plays are presented from time to time at NJPAC, Newark Symphony Hall, or the various schools and colleges. Ethnic festivals are featured during warm weather and there are many parades. Ethnic restaurants vie with each other in the Ironbound section, and several upscale restaurants are located in the center city. Games are featured at the new Bears and Eagles Riverfront Stadium, the Schools Stadium, Untermann Field, Weequahic Park, and fields in the county and city parks. There are numerous tennis courts and swimming pools in the city and Weequahic Park has an 18-hole golf course.

9. HERE TO SERVE

Rivalry between the Town of Newark and Elizabethtown was on-going over the years. Elizabethtown, settled first, considered itself superior to Newark. Elizabethtown was the first English-speaking settlement in New Jersey and the first state capital. It was also the largest community until the Revolutionary War, and many of the Province's and state's leaders came from Elizabethtown.

Elizabethtown felt that the county courthouse should be in within its boundaries. Newark, then the largest municipality in the state, believed that the courthouse should be located in Newark. Finally, after much discussion, a three-day referendum was held on Day's Hill (located near the former Olympic Park in Irvington) and the Center of Newark. The election is called the most corrupt in the state's history. Under the 1776 constitution, all persons were able to vote if they were 21 years old and possessed 50 pounds worth of property. This included African Americans and women. Everyone voted in the 1807 election, not once but two, three, or four times—even the former citizens in the graveyards cast a vote. When the votes were counted, Newark won.

The state legislature in the 1844 constitution took the vote away from women, blacks, and foreigners as a result of the 1807 election, meaning only free, white males, 21 years old with at least 50 pounds worth of property, could vote. Black men gained the vote in 1875, and women had to wait until 1920.

The borough courthouse in Elizabeth continued to function for local cases, and it became the site of the Union County Courthouse in 1857. Moses Miller Crane, a Democrat, who objected strongly to women voting, spearheaded the movement to form Union County. It was the 21st and last county to be organized in New Jersey. Crane is known as the father of Union County.

Newark's water supply originally came from the streams flowing through the hamlet or wells dug near the homes. The Passaic River was an especially good source of water until it became too polluted with factory and household waste. The new sewers in Newark, Passaic, and Paterson carried waste directly into the river. The early industrialization of the communities and the heavy use of chemicals on farmlands increased the pollution and made them unsafe to use. Diseases were rampant, especially typhoid fever, dysentery, and diarrhea.

The city built at least two reservoirs for pure water. One was built in 1872 by the Newark Aqueduct Board at the southern end of the future Branch Brook Park. Another was constructed on South Orange Avenue near Springfield Avenue. The city fathers looked for a new water supply and found it in the Pequannock River and its tributaries. The City of Newark acquired some 35,000 acres in the Pequannock Watershed in Passaic, Morris, and Sussex Counties. Dams were built at Oak Ridge, Echo Lake, Clinton, Macopin, and Canistear. The State of New Jersey has protected nearly 9,000 acres through purchase or easements.

Seven municipalities joined to build the Wanaque Reservoir in addition to Newark in 1907. They were Paterson, Passaic, Clifton, Montclair, Bloomfield, Glen Ridge, and Kearny, and it was completed in 1920. As a result, Newark has one of the best water systems in New Jersey because it is free of chemicals, salt, and gasoline from public streets, farmlands, or industries. The pure water is carried to the cities it serves in pipes from the reservoirs instead of being taken from the adjacent streams with raw sewage.

However, as the cities spread out and people began to move into the countryside, the watershed has been threatened by developers for subdivisions for residences, shopping malls, and amphitheaters. Numerous citizen groups, such as Passaic County, the Highlands Coalition, West Milford, Jefferson and Rockaway Township, Butler, Bloomingdale, and Kinnelon Boroughs, voice objections to further development around the watershed. Newark, with much untaxable property, seeks to develop some of the watershed.

During the Revolutionary War, there were no hospitals. Schools such as the Lyons Farms School or churches such as Trinity Episcopal were used briefly for injured or sick soldiers, but no regular facility was established. Newark's first hospital was the Marcus Ward Hospital during the Civil War, started by Marcus Ward, "the soldier's friend." Organized in a warehouse in 1862, it was used until 1865, when the war ended.

St. Barnabas Hospital, operated by the Episcopal Church, opened in 1867. The first building, located on Avon Avenue at St. Mark's Place, was used until the City put a street through the site. The hospital selected a plot on High Street at Montgomery Street. A cornerstone was laid for a new building at the site in 1884, and the facility was opened in May 1885. At first, the Ladies Society of St. Barnabas had charge of the nursing duties. In 1875, they were replaced by the Sisterhood of Saint Elizabeth, who in turn were replaced by the Sisters of Saint Margaret, Episcopalian nuns. The maternity and children's wards were opened in 1877. A nurses' training school was established in 1895, and the nuns were later replaced by regular nurses. The hospital moved to Livingston in 1964, and since that time, has absorbed many of the area hospitals, including United Hospitals, Beth Israel Medical Center, Irvington General Hospital, and Union Memorial Hospital.

The St. Michael's Medical Center began in a house on Bleeker Street and greatly expanded.

The first and second sections of St. Michael's Hospital on High Street (Martin Luther King Boulevard) were completed in 1871 and 1888. Both were designed by Jeremiah O'Rourke, who also was the architect of Sacred Heart Basilica and the razed St. James Roman Catholic Church. The exterior is red brick and has several gables, a mansard roof, stone lintels, and Gothic arched entrance. A modern addition and parking lot were placed on the University Avenue side of the building in the 1980s.

The Newark Charitable Eye and Ear Infirmary to prevent blindness in infants was founded by Dr. Charles Kipp in 1880. It became part of the United Hospitals Medical Center on South Ninth Street in April 1969, and has been absorbed by the St. Barnabas Medical Center. The Dr. Henry C. Barkhorn Memorial Hearing and Speech Center, a project of the Newark Eye and Ear Infirmary, opened at 136 Plane Street in January 1959. It was designed to provide help for those with speech or hearing impediments without duplicating the clinical services already available.

The Newark City Hospital began in 1881. It became the Martland Medical Center after Dr. Harrison A. Martland discovered the workers who painted the dials of watches in a factory in Orange suffered danger of radiation. The color barrier which had helped to ban both physicians and patients from hospitals was broken in 1946, when Dr. Mae McCarroll and Dr. Clarence Janifer became the

By 1914, the Newark City Hospital had purchased its second motorized ambulance. The Board of Health operated this vehicle and service.

first African-American physicians to be added to the staff. At that time, it was necessary to be a member of the American Medical Association (AMA) to practice at Martland and AMA didn't permit black members, according to Dr. McCarroll in a 1984 interview. She applied for membership annually until she was accepted. When she was appointed, the hospital also opened its doors to African-American girls who desired to attend its nursing school.

Dr. McCarroll came to Newark in 1929 as the wife of Dr. LeRoy Baxter, a dentist, future assemblyman, and son of James Baxter, principal of the Newark Colored School in 1866. The hospital became University Hospital and part of the University of Medicine and Dentistry. The (Dr. Aaron) Haskin-McCarroll Public Health Building was dedicated to her in 1982. She was cited as the "First Lady" of the National Medical Association (NMA), the professional organization of black physicians. She later divorced Baxter and married Robert Hunter, an officer in the Howard Savings Bank.

The Newark German Hospital (Clara Maass Memorial Hospital in Belleville) started in 1868. Clara Maass, a graduate of its nurses' training school, allowed herself to be bitten by a mosquito in Cuba during the Spanish-American War, contracted malaria, and died on August 24, 1901. Her experiment helped to solve the spread of the disease. The hospital was renamed the Newark Memorial Hospital in 1919, then the Lutheran Memorial Hospital in 1946, and finally became the Clara Maass Memorial Hospital in 1952. The facility was moved to a site adjacent to Branch Brook Park on the Belleville-Newark line in 1957.

Dr. Henry L. Coit spearheaded the crusade for pure milk. He also established the Baby Keep Well Stations to help mothers keep healthy babies well by having periodic checkups. His activities resulted in the founding of the Babies Hospital Coit Memorial in 1896. It later became the Babies Unit of United Hospitals Medical Center, and since 1999, it has been located at Beth Israel Medical Center on Lyons Avenue as part of St. Barnabas Medical Center.

The Roseville Benevolent Society, which sewed for the poor, realized there was a lack of facilities for crippled and maimed children. The women rented a four-room flat on 66 South Eighth Street for the makeshift hospital. Later, quarters were built at 89 Park Avenue, and it was incorporated as the Hospital and Home for Crippled Children.

St. James Hospital was founded adjacent to St. James Roman Catholic Church in 1900. In 1961, it moved into a new building at 155 Jefferson Street. The church subsequently was razed to make way for a parking lot for the hospital. The hospital was administered for many years by the Sisters of St. Joseph. It serves residents of the Ironbound section as well as emergencies at Newark International Airport, Port Newark, and local factories.

The Beth Israel Hospital was started by the Hebrew Hospital and Dispensary Association and the Daughters of Israel Hospital Association. Chartered on October 25, 1901, the group acquired an old Victorian house on High Street at West Kinney Street, which opened as Beth Israel Hospital on September 8, 1901. The new facility immediately started a fund-raising campaign for a new building, which was dedicated on January 19, 1908, with 80 beds. Almost immediately, the

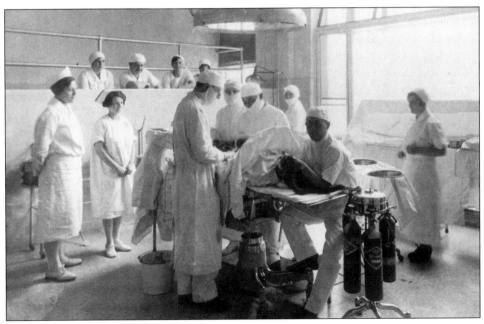

Doctors at Beth Israel Hospital perform an operation in the Lyons Avenue facility.

This is the Presbyterian Hospital, which became a part of United Hospitals.

new structure was overcrowded and new quarters were needed. The board found a former farm on Lyons Avenue at Osborne Terrace used for carnivals as the new site, and it was opened on February 19, 1928, less than 20 years after its first building. In 1931, the Newark Maternity Hospital (serving the community from 1912 to 1931) was amalgamated with the Beth. The quarters of the Newark Maternity Hospital on High Street were used by the Home for Incurables and Convalescents, founded in 1881, after the maternity group joined the Beth.

The Homeopathic Hospital apparently joined the East Orange General Hospital in the 1920s, while the Presbyterian Hospital became a part of the United Hospital. The American Legion Hospital at 741 Broadway started after World War I and operated until 1953, when it closed because of lack of funds.

Columbus Hospital was incorporated in 1934 by a group of Italian businessmen who wanted a hospital where Italian doctors could practice. The 210-bed hospital was built at 495 North Thirteenth Street in the North Ward in a heavily Italian neighborhood. In 1999, it joined the Cathedral Health Care System, which included St. Michael's and St. James Hospitals (both in Newark), St. Mary's Life Center (Orange), and Hospital Center (Orange). Today, there are five hospitals in Newark: University Hospital, affiliated with the University of Medicine and Dentistry; Beth Israel Medical Center, affiliated with St. Barnabas Health Care System (Livingston); Columbus Hospital; St. Michael's Hospital; and St. James Hospital. The Mount Carmel Guild Hospital, at 1160 Raymond Boulevard in Newark, is devoted to comprehensive in-patient and out-patient services for mental illness and substance abuse only.

When the influenza epidemic struck Newark in September 1918, the hospitals were quickly filled over their capacity limits. Mayor Charles P. Gillen had a vacant building on Broad Street and Central Avenue turned into an emergency hospital. Some 1,133 died by the time the epidemic ceased in November. Evergreen Cemetery on the Elizabeth-Hillside-Newark border recorded 1,800 burials of flu victims from those three communities.

Dr. John A. Kenney founded New Jersey's first and only all-black hospital in 1927, where African Americans could intern and serve as physicians. He named the hospital at 132 West Kinney Street for his father and operated it until January 1, 1935, when he donated it to the Booker T. Washington Community Hospital Association of Newark. Three days later, it was incorporated as the Community Hospital of Newark. Located in the old Third Ward, or "the Hill," section of the city, the hospital had beds for 34 patients. Adjacent to the hospital was a frame building with an additional 16 rooms and space for an administrative center. The Community Hospital existed for only another 17 years, but served about 4,500 patients in that time. Amazingly, only 19 deaths were recorded. Dr. Kenney formed a consulting staff composed of some of the most outstanding white physicians in Newark. The hospital closed in 1953. The building was then purchased by the New Salem Baptist Church to serve the spiritual needs of the community.

In 1943, the athletic field containing the tennis courts and running track facilities in Weequahic Park was replaced by a hospital and housing for the United States Army Air Corps. In addition, doctors on the staff at Beth Israel Hospital who were not called into service were organized to man the hospital after the

Dressed in street-length uniforms, these two nurses worked at the Newark City Hospital in 1903.

The men of Hook and Ladder Company Number 5 pose in front of their building with their equipment and team of horses.

anticipated invasion of Europe on D-Day, when the military expected heavy casualties. The doctors purchased their own uniforms, brushed up on the types of wounds they believed they would be treating, and waited to be called—they never were. When the time came, those who were injured were returned to England for treatment. Only one physician was called to deliver a baby for a soldier's wife. At the war's end, the complex was turned into temporary housing for returning servicemen.

Fire was one of the biggest concerns of the residents of Newark. Lightning or a faulty flue in a fireplace or a high wind could carry sparks to a haystack, a barn, or a rooftop and destroy it. Every householder in early Newark was required to keep two leather buckets and a ladder handy in case there was a fire. The two buckets were insufficient to fight a major fire, but if the schoolhouse and church bells or the fire gong rang, enough of the men and boys would form a bucket brigade from the nearest well, spring, pond, or stream. When insurance companies were formed, plaques were placed on insured houses to indicate that the water should be poured on them. Unfortunately, this did not work because fire has a tendency to spread to the adjacent buildings.

There was no formal firefighting team until fire demolished the home of Judge Elisha Boudinot on Park Place in January 1797. Reverend Dr. Alexander Macwhorter and Reverend Uzal Ogden called a mass meeting of the people of the town to ask for the formation of a volunteer fire department. They also urged the purchase of a hand pumper.

The fire pumpers originally were pulled by the volunteers. The bucket brigade could pour the water into the pumper and men would pump the handle to activate the hose's stream of water. From about 1815 to 1864, the pumpers could both take water in and pour it out. A partially-paid department was started while some men were "on call" in 1854. In addition, the watchmen who patrolled the streets at night were directed to watch out for possible fires.

Later, fire hydrants were installed along the streets, but they provided insufficient water for two disastrous fires: one from a boarding house on Market Street and the other on Broad Street, which threatened the Trinity Episcopal Church. Finally, fire hydrants were placed all within distance of inner city buildings. Pumpers operated by little steam engines were introduced about 1862. The steam engine contained four hoses and could pour 600 gallons of a water on a fire per minute.

The Newark Salvage Corps was organized in 1879 and continued until 1951 under the Underwriters Protective Association. The corp's job was to attempt to protect furniture and other property from fire and water damage. Each man carried large waterproof canvases, which they were directed to throw over furniture to protect it from the blaze. These men also moved contents of a property from the path of the fire if possible and secured the building against additional damage of wind and weather after the fire was extinguished by the firemen.

Gasoline-powered automobiles were introduced to the Newark Fire Department in 1906, and by 1911, they were installed in the fire engines.

145

These firemen are patrolling the Passaic River's waterfront aboard the fire boat Renaissance *in 1992.*

A fire alarm system was installed in 1870. The department was organized in 1889 as a paid department. Motorized vehicles began replacing horses by 1911, and all horses were replaced by December 20, 1923. The recruits began receiving formal instructions of fighting fires in 1911.

Firehouses are strategically located throughout the city for efficient and quick response time. Fire boats patrol the Passaic River and Newark Bay. The extensive use of diverse chemicals in manufacturing and in home products has made firefighting more dangerous than it was when the items burning were merely wood, hay, or cloth. The local department's success in containing fires has become legendary in Newark. Fire prevention programs and fire inspection of schools, factories, and office and public buildings are routine.

Dedicated on June 13, 1888, the Firemen's Monument in Mount Pleasant Cemetery marks the Firemen's Burial Plot in the cemetery. The plot was acquired by the local fire department in 1855 and was fenced in April 1870 with two granite posts at the gate. One of the posts is named in honor of Chief Engineer Ellis R. Carhuff, who encouraged the project. "Chief Engineer" was the name given to the fire chief until April 1967.

Upon settlement in the late 1600s, Newark had a curfew. Nobody was permitted on the street after dark. A night watch patrolled the area to make certain that there were no prowlers about the town. When the town became a city, Mayor William Halsey appointed a "Watch and Lamp District" of the new city to patrol the streets and alleys and apprehend all suspicious persons lurking in them.

Leather caps were provided for the watch to identify the members. In 1844, these leather caps were also provided for the mayor, the city marshall, constables, and finally the police magistrates. In 1857, the charter was amended to consolidate the watchmen and the constables under the chief of police. In 1860, the police were directed to wear a blue coat with police buttons, uniform, cap, and star. A building behind city hall on William Street became the first police station in 1864. Their equipment was increased to include night sticks. The police department acquired its first automobile for patrol in 1910.

The organization of the department has changed as the city government has changed. There have been eight different forms of government. The present form is a strong mayor and council composed of representatives of each of the five wards and four at large. A police trailer is located at the Four Corners and each precinct has a full complement of officers.

Crime, which had escalated as property owners became absentee owners and failed to maintain the property or pay their taxes, has decreased over recent years. Neglected lots have been cleared. High-rise apartments that were constructed just before or after World War II for the poor and which had became havens for drug addicts are being removed and replaced by low two- or three-story housing built by both the public and private sector.

On a traffic island in the middle of Broad Street, a tall tower stood at the Four Corners until 1937, when it was removed to Clinton Cemetery in Clinton. The tower gave police a better view of activities along the street.

The present Newark City Hall was erected in 1906 and features a magnificent gold dome.

A former hotel on Broad and William Street served as a the city hall in 1864 and it was replaced by the present attractive building in 1906. A year later, a new courthouse, now the Hall of Records, at the intersection of Springfield and West Market Streets, was dedicated, and it replaced an earlier building erected in 1838.

Newark's Human Services building on University Avenue at William Street, dedicated in June 1990, was named for the late Earl L. Harris Sr., a former city council president, who died in 1988. According to Mayor Sharpe James, "Harris stood for giving hope to the hopeless." He praised Harris for fighting the Essex County Board of Freeholders so that Essex County College would remain in Newark, for authoring Newark's rent control bill, and for introducing the Meals on Wheels program, which provides food, financial and rent subsidies, payment of hospital bills, and rehabilitation treatment.

Newarkers in the nineteenth century feared and distrusted the unknown. They were suspicious of strangers who spoke different languages, had different customs, dressed differently, enjoyed different music, and attended a different house of worship. However, over time, Newark citizens began embracing their diversity and ceased to focus exclusively on one nationality or religion. Hospitals began accepting patients from the entire population and the other public service agencies in Newark also evolved so that people of all ethnic groups were included in their work.

10. RENEWAL, RESTORATION, AND REVIVAL

Several organizations and individuals have refused to leave Newark. The Cathedral of the Sacred Heart, which stands high above its neighbors on a hill adjacent to Branch Brook Park, became a basilica when visited by Pope John Paul II in October 1995. The Beth Israel Hospital, located on a hill high above Weequahic Park and clearly visible to all airplanes landing at Newark International Airport, decided to remain in the city in 1964, even after a large percentage of the Jewish population had moved from the city.

McCarter and English, Newark's oldest law firm, moved into the new Law Center and decided its future would continue to be in the city where it began in 1865. The Prudential Insurance Company, a landmark in the city, continues to be one of the main supporters of Newark's recovery. The company's management decided that its future would continue to be in the city.

St. Benedict's College, established in 1868 by German monks, ceased operations during World War I, but the secondary preparatory school continued. Many boys of German, Irish, and Italian descent from Newark and its suburbs attended the prep school. After the riot in 1967, the school was closed for a year while the Benedictine Brothers, who operated it, decided what to do. They reopened, determined to teach the youth of Newark and suburbs. The students now are primarily African American, Hispanic, and Portuguese. A new school kindergarten through eighth grade is being built on the academy's 14-acre site for St. Mary's School.

While Mount Prospect Country Day School, a private school for girls in the old Clark Mansion in the North Ward, closed, St. Vincent's Academy for girls on West Market Street decided to remain open. Several small private schools have opened since the riot. Some are related to churches; among them are the 1998 St. James Preparatory School on Court Street; Calvary Gospel Church School, built in 1971, on Lyons Avenue at Elizabeth Avenue; and the North Star Academy and St Philip's Academy, both on Washington Place.

In the meantime, the Newark Public Library and its near neighbor, the Newark Museum, continued to serve the public. The library is a resource center for people throughout the state, while the membership of the museum stretches across the Hudson River to the five boroughs of New York City, as well as to communities throughout New Jersey. It is considered to be one of the finest small museums in the nation.

The New Jersey Symphony Hall, built as a mosque for the Salaam Temple in 1925, and later taken over by the City, is a refurbished concert hall featuring world-renowned musicians, dancers, and entertainers since NJPAC opened in October 1997. Audiences come from throughout the state and New York City. A loop bus carries them with stops at Penn and Lackawanna Stations, both restored. The bus also stops at other places such as the library and museum.

Two groups, Friends of Branch Brook Park and the newer Friends of Weequahic Park, are endeavoring to make the two parks the showplaces they once were. Work also is progressing on Riverbank Park as part of the restoration of the Passaic River shoreline in conjunction with the construction of the New Jersey Performing Arts Center.

The New Jersey Historical Society, after more than seven decades on Broadway, relocated to the Essex Club building on Park Place near NJPAC in 1997. The Robert Treat Hotel, one of the city's best, has opened a new dining room, and several other new restaurants also are located in the vicinity to serve NJPAC audiences.

The Public Service Electric and Gas Company razed its former building on Park Place and constructed a new one behind it on Raymond Boulevard. The Park Place frontage now features a fountain and amphitheater, where concerts are presented. The street in front frequently closes for a variety of ethnic festivals.

Five colleges have shown their faith in the city's future by enlarging their campuses. Independent investors are restoring old office buildings. The city's two tallest buildings—the Lefcourt Building on Commerce Street and the National Newark and Essex Building at 750 Broad Street—have been remodeled as a college dormitory and office building, respectively.

The Firemen's Insurance Company building near NJPAC has been renovated, and the New Jersey Telephone Company, now Verizon, also has been refurbished. Plans are on the drawing board for redevelopment of the area on Broad Street from Hahne's Department Store building and the Griffith Building to Central Avenue for residences, business offices, convenience stores, restaurants, and shops.

The facade of the South Park Presbyterian Church was saved from demolition because of its beauty, and flowers are planted in front of it every spring. The rest of the building, then being used as a shelter for the homeless, was destroyed by fire. The shelter, the Lighthouse Gospel Mission, relocated to nearby Washington Street.

A portion of the Wickliffe Presbyterian Church, once known as the Thirteenth Avenue Presbyterian Church and said to be the first "colored" church in the city, still stands in the Hovnanian "Society Hill" complex in University Heights as a reminder of the past.

Several church groups have formed housing corporations to redevelop the city. The most successful and largest of these is the New Community Corporation (NCC), formed in the spring of 1968. This group hosted a walk in the Central Ward for facilitating understanding by people from the suburbs. The Right Reverend Monsignor William Linder, now pastor of St. Rose of Lima Roman Catholic Church, surveyed the parishioners as to their needs and desires. Out of the survey grew the NCC, which has erected 18 housing developments in Newark, Jersey City, and Englewood containing 3,000 apartments for 8,000 residents. NCC also has refurbished a former hotel and nunnery for senior citizen housing. The new 206 town houses are sold to low-income persons.

NCC provides all sorts of services to the Newark community. These include an employment service center, a federal credit union, an extended care facility with 180 beds plus day care for 100 clients, transitional housing for 102 homeless families, a center for employment training, and a youth automotive training center. Its corporate offices at St. Joseph's Plaza, a former church, also contain a sandwich shop, conference and banquet facilities, and a restaurant. The Pathmark Shopping Center, built by NCC, features several fast-food restaurants. There are two charter schools and a recreation center. It will continue to explore economic opportunities for urban residents so that they may leave welfare and enter the world of work, to create small businesses, and to improve employee skills.

New Community Corporation continues to build new structures in Newark. This high rise under construction is called New Community Commons, a residence for senior citizens.

This block of two- and three-story homes is for New Community families. In more recent years, the dwellings are being sold to the occupants.

Babyland Family Services Inc., started by Mary P. Smith in August 1969, provides care for more than 1,500 children at 12 facilities. Eight of these are child care centers for children ranging from three months to five years. The Babyland Domestic Violence Shelter, established in 1979, provides 24-hour crisis intervention for victims of family violence. There is a counseling service for suburban residents in Livingston. The Children Together Foster Care Program, initiated in 1993, keeps siblings together in foster homes or reunites them with family members. The program also offers an emergency shelter, a course to train foster parents, and instruction in care of boarder babies.

St. Rose of Lima School is training children in a strong academic curriculum and providing after-school care. The NCC Foundation is providing scholarships for elementary and secondary students to attend the schools.

New Visions Community Development Corporation, an outgrowth of Unity Freedom Church, built 30 houses on the Newark-Irvington border. St. James AME Church owns St. James Towers, the 220-unit apartment building on Washington Street. The church also has a federal credit union and wellness center. The Metropolitan United Ministries Development Corporation has completed four projects in the Central Ward containing 150 new houses with 114 affordable housing units.

Several other groups with the cooperation of the City are also active. Formed in 1950, the Leaguers Educational and Cultural Center at 731 Clinton Avenue provides educational and recreational programs for youth. Each year it conducts a debutant ball for the young women in the group. Programs are both tutorial and recreational. Several Head Start programs are offered for pre-school children, and various scholarships are awarded for college.

Nellie Grier, known lovingly as "Mother Grier," started the Emanuel Senior Citizens Day Care Center and was an organizer of the Newark Senior Citizens Council to help the handicapped elderly get out of their homes, get nutritious meals, and get access to medical services. The center at 98–104 Maple Avenue was renamed the Mother Nellie Grier Senior Citizens Center in 1984. The seniors are picked up at their homes each morning and taken to the center, where they associate with their peers for several hours, eat, and then are returned to their homes.

Newark developed into a city of neighborhoods. Each area, in many aspects, was almost a city unto itself with businesses, stores, schools, and churches. Woodside, the area so aptly named near the Belleville line, became Forest Hill, where a historic district of some 2,000 homes has been set aside. Woodside was a wooded area until it was subdivided late in the nineteenth century. More suburban than urban, Forest Hill was developed as an upscale one-family section with large wooden frame and brick houses. One of the most magnificent residences is the mansion that belonged to Madam Maria Jeritza, the opera star.

The Ironbound section, once known as Dutch and Irish Necks because of the people who lived there, continues to be the first home for immigrants as they arrive in Newark. Today, there are many Hispanic and Portuguese families. The word "Ironbound" refers to the area's being bound by railroad tracks. This area has been called home by a variety of ethnic groups, including African Americans, Germans, Hispanics, Irish, Jews, Portuguese, Polish, Lithuanians, and Central Europeans.

Once the home for factory workers, the Ironbound continues to be a home for persons who love the area, one of the safest in the city. Ferry Street, the main shopping street, is crowded daily as customers browse for everything they need in small shops, many still family-owned. Cafes and delis crowd the area, while

Children hold hands as they take a walk with one of the caregivers at Babyland Day Nursery in Newark. Mary Smith organized the nurseries in 1969.

Emilio Serio, whose home and studio are located in the Ironbound section, sits in front of a painting he created for the New Jersey Opera's production of Tosca *in 1992.*

upper-class restaurants have become a haven for people from the suburbs who seek delicious Portuguese or Spanish dinners.

In the 1970s, several artists moved into empty factory lofts. Some have continued to stay there. Troy West, an architectural professor at NJIT, is one of the residents. Emilio Serio's art studio is located at 30 Houston Street in a former parochial school. This building was erected originally as a school in 1879 and served, in turns, as a tinsmith's shop, a Greek Catholic church, a social club, and a Polish National Catholic church before Serio purchased it in 1970 and transformed the wooden building into a studio and home. In 1978, Attorney Anthony Cabelo purchased another area church, the Christ Episcopal Church at 75 Prospect Street, designed by Frank Wills in 1849–1850, after a fire and remodeled it into an office and home. The Conmar Zipper factory on Thomas Street was razed and 50 one-family dwellings with two or three bedrooms erected; the $8,950,000 development is scheduled for completion in 2002. Other residents, although they may work out of the area, are the third generation to live in the Ironbound section. While the houses continue to have the same appearance as they did a half century or century ago, many of them sport new siding and have been updated inside.

The Roseville section, settled around 1880, frequently was the first residential section the people in the center city moved to as they left the city. This area contained many churches of the major denominations, including St. Rose of Lima Roman Catholic Church.

Vailsburg, a farm area, was part of South Orange until 1894, when it became the Borough of Vailsburg. It joined the City of Newark in 1905, but has considered separating from the city from time to time. South Orange Avenue is its main street, which is lined with churches and stores. Vailsburg is adjacent to Seton Hall

University, and the area includes Vailsburg Park. A farmhouse, the last one in the area, at 283 Stuyvesant Avenue and Schofield Street, was restored and six new houses were built on the 65-acre site called Farmhouse Commons. Started in 1995, the project was completed by the Unified Vailsburg Services.

Clinton Hill attracted well-to-do people at the turn of the twentieth century. Clinton Avenue contains several beautiful churches, including the Temple B'nai Abraham, which moved to Livingston, and Blessed Sacrament School, Rectory, and Church.

Weequahic section was the last to be developed. Work in Meeker Avenue began in a subdivision by the Weequahic Development Company in 1910. Most of the early dwellings were one-family residences. Soon two families were added, and in the 1920s, apartments were built along Elizabeth Avenue. The apartments attracted a large Jewish population after 1920. They stayed for about 40 years until they too followed their neighbors to the suburbs. Other small shopping areas developed near the Irvington line on Chancellor and Lyons Avenues. A prosperous shopping area developed on Bergen Street with food, clothing, banks, a movie theater, and sweet shops. Originally, Weequahic was part of Lyons Farms and later Clinton Township. Until subdivisions began to develop, the area remained primarily farmland.

The city has several historic districts where the property owners have lovingly restored their buildings. One of these, between the library and museum, is James Street Commons, a collection of brownstone townhouses with tiny vest pocket gardens, all restored to their original splendor. Ari Hovnanian has built the attractive University Heights section on Society Hill above Martin Luther King Boulevard. Many of the occupants are people who moved from Newark but returned because they love the city and the development is closer to friends and family or their jobs.

In the meantime, a large demolition project has been on-going. Burned-out, neglected, vandalized buildings and hard-to-police high rises are being removed to make way for one- or two-story individual units. Garbage and debris have been removed from vacant lots and graffiti has been washed off or painted over on walls—all to give the city a cleaner and neater appearance. Empty lots have been fenced to make it difficult to dump tires and other items into them.

All, however, is not perfect in Newark. The city suffers from the same urban decay found in many of the nation's older cities. After 1920, many factory owners moved from the city. Some of them lost interest in their properties when their buildings became out-moded and staffs were reduced. In many cases, the buildings were abandoned and then became the victims of crimes, including arson—frequently for the insurance money. Drug addicts used them as hangouts. Much of the housing is old and unmaintained. When the owners were unable to collect rents on the dwellings, they abandoned them instead of bringing them up to code. Many structures have been seized by the City and razed.

For six days, from July 12 to July 17, 1967, the city was rocked by a riot initially caused by the arrest of an African-American taxi driver on motor violations. The arrest on a hot day was accompanied by numerous rumors when several witnesses saw him carried into a district police station. Efforts to calm a crowd of about 250 persons who gathered outside the police headquarters failed. At 11:36 p.m., someone threw a Molotov cocktail (an urban guerrilla bomb) against the precinct's wall, the first ever thrown in Newark.

The protests grew out of frustrations of poor substandard housing, unemployment, a failed anti-poverty program, inferior educational opportunities, unkept promises from politicians, a general lack of respect, and failure to have African Americans and Hispanics in leadership roles in government, the police and fire departments, educational institutions, and industry and commerce. These concerns and issues were common in the black communities in Plainfield and Englewood in New Jersey, as well as throughout the nation after World War II.

Meetings were conducted on Thursday, July 13, in hopes of solving the problems. An anonymously written leaflet protesting police brutality was distributed and calls for a mass rally were issued. There was some looting and vandalism in all parts of the city. By 2:30 a.m. on Friday, July 14, local officials decided to call Governor Richard Hughes and ask for help from the state police and National Guard. The assisting officers and soldiers made their headquarters at the Roseville Armory, and the Schools Stadium provided camp space for the guardsmen. Teams were composed of local police, guardsmen, and state police, and they set up blockades at 137 intersections leading into the city and 19 checkpoints. Traffic was prohibited between 10 p.m. and 6 a.m. and there was a curfew for people from 11 p.m. to 6 a.m. No alcoholic beverages, narcotics, or explosives could be sold. The city was sealed off.

The various law enforcement agencies were unable to communicate with each other by radio because each one was on a different frequency. In several instances, it was discovered that various units were shooting at one another. Some officers and guardsmen were charged with deliberately shooting out show windows of black businesses. On Sunday, emergency food was brought into the city for distribution to people in the riot area, determined to be Springfield Avenue near High Street. Only food stores, restaurants, banks, and public utilities were opened on Monday, July 17. All other businesses were closed. On Tuesday, July 18, all businesses were reopened and the troops left the city.

Twenty-six people died. Of these, two were city employees: Fire Captain Michael Moran and Detective Fred Toto. Captain Moran died at a fire. The fire department received more than 364 calls during the riot, of which 64 were false and 50 were non-fire related. Detective Fred Toto was shot. One woman had a heart attack and died on Thursday, another suffered a fractured pelvis and died when her car struck a fire engine on Wednesday, and one man died of an overdose of narcotics on Sunday.

The Governor's Select Commission on Civil Disorder in the State of New Jersey conducted an extensive investigation. Among its conclusions were that the state police be notified immediately in case of trouble and be placed in charge at the scene and that all radios be on the same frequency. It also recommended sensitivity training for law enforcement officers and efforts to provide real equality for African Americans from landlords, shop stewards, employers, shopkeepers, social workers, and public employees. Law and order must prevail, the report noted, in conditions of social justice. Numerous suggestions followed concerning actions at a disturbance and proposals for recreation, health, welfare, schools, and employment.

In 1972, the City was considering selling some of its land in the Pequannock Watershed, which supplied about half of the city's water—the other half comes from the Wanaque Reservoir. Developers sought to put strip malls along the highways, people wanted to live in the watershed area, and others wanted more recreational facilities, such as skiing. Considered to be one of the last frontiers in New Jersey, conservationists want the land to stay as it is.

Newark, with much tax exempt land, is eager to find another source of income. The federal, state, and city buildings, five colleges, public and private schools, and the many houses of worship in Newark all are tax exempt, while still needing city services. The public elementary and high schools schools once considered to be the best in the state were taken over by the State in 1995. Unfortunately, the bookkeeping was so poor that the State estimates that some money is missing. Most of the schools are quite old and many need repairs.

Newark has been much maligned by humorists and the press. In the motion picture *Golden Boy*, starring William Holden and Barbara Stanwyck, Miss Stanwyck's character, a tough fight promoter's moll, remarks to Holden, "I'm just a Babe from Newark." When the 30th anniversary of the tragic riot in Newark was approaching in July 1997, Charles F. Cummings, the city historian, was flooded with telephone calls from the national media seeking information on the city 30 years later—and the fact that Newark had been dubbed the car theft capital of America, didn't help.

This is a bird's-eye view of the Newark's Gateway Complex, train station, and Law and Communications Center.

Several Newark groups are doing their best to eliminate that idea. Police work has helped to reduce the number of stolen cars so the city no longer leads the nation. Crime has been decreased by a larger police presence. The concert halls, museum, library, new baseball stadium, insurance companies, airport, federal and county offices, the colleges, and building contractors who are willing to invest in rehabilitating old office buildings are all attracting people to the city once again. Both the old Lackawanna and Penn Stations have been restored. A special loop bus has been added to the regular bus service, making it easier to get around mid-town. Upscale restaurants and auxiliary stores are returning to the business center. The former American Insurance Company, which served as Rutgers Law School, is scheduled to become an urban city hotel. The streets are clean and well-lighted—the staple of any good city.

Mayor Kenneth Gibson, Newark's first African-American mayor, observed once that if anything happened, Newark would get there first. Gibson meant the unfortunate plight that the city was in at that time. Now, however, there is only one way for the city to go and that is up. From all appearances, it is doing just that.

Newark, the third oldest American city, has had its ups and downs. Its location attracted people in search of a better life. The goal was possible, but for many it was not easy. It took 200 years to reach Newark's golden age of huge factories and grand mansions. The Great Depression, World Wars I and II, outmoded factories, and housing stock abandoned by absentee landlords caused unnecessary detours found in most old cities. However, throughout its history, there have been many people, businesses, and organizations that have shared a basic faith in the city. Newark faces the twenty-first century with hope as old town houses and Art Deco buildings are restored, abandoned housing is removed and replaced by modern homes, new businesses move in, and people who fled the city return.

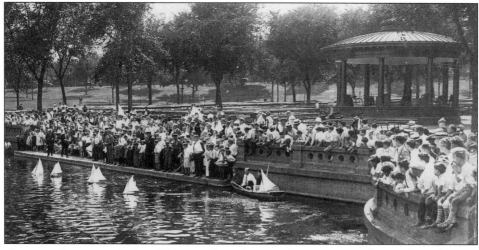

Among a large crowd, the children sailing their toy boats in Branch Brook Park recall Newark's romantic days of old.

SELECTED BIBLIOGRAPHY

Atkinson, James. *History of Newark*. William B. Guild, 1878.

Conniff, James C.G., and Richard Conniff. *A History of PSE&G: The Energy People*. Newark: Public Service Electric and Gas Company, 1978.

Cross, Dorothy. *Indians of New Jersey*. New Jersey Historical Society, 1952.

Cunningham, Barbara. *The New Jersey Ethnic Experience*. Union City: William H. Wise and Co., 1976.

Cunningham, John T. *New Jersey's Main Road*. New York: Doubleday and Co., 1966.

———. *New Jersey: A Mirror on America*. Florham Park: Afton Publishing Company, 1988.

———. *Newark*. Newark: New Jersey Historical Society, 1966 and 1988.

Cunningham, John, and Charles Cummings. *Remembering Essex*. Virginia Beach: Donning, 1995.

Ellison, Harry C. *Church of the Founding Fathers of New Jersey*. Cornish, Maine: Carbrook Press, 1964.

Hagaman, Adaline. *Early New Jersey*. New York University Publishing Co., 1964.

Jenkinson, Richard C. *Old South High Street*. Newark: Newark Public Library, 1929.

Kennedy, John F. *A Nation of Immigrants*. New York: Harper and Row, 1964.

Kobbe, Gustave. *The Central Railroad of New Jersey*. New York: Central Railroad of New Jersey, 1890.

Lane, Wheaton J. *From Indian Trails to Iron Horse*. Princeton: Princeton University Press, 1939.

McCormick, Richard P. *Experiment in Independence, New Jersey in the Critical Period, 1781–1789*. New Jersey Historical Series. Newark: D. Van Nostrand Company, 1964

McCormick, Richard P. *New Jersey from Colony to State, 1609–1789*. New Jersey Historical Series. Newark: D. Van Nostrand Company, 1964.

Miers, Earl Schenck. *Crossroad of Freedom*. New Brunswick, Rutgers University Press, 1971.

Newark Museum. *A Survey: 50 Years of the Newark Museum*. Newark: Newark Museum, 1959.

Pomfret, John E. *The Province of East Jersey, 1609–1702: The Rebellious Proprietary*. Princeton, Princeton University Press, 1962.

Shaw, William H. *History of Essex and Hudson Counties, N.J.* Everts and Peck, 1884.

Urquhart, Frank J. *History of Newark, 1666–1913*. Lewis Historical Publishing Co., 1913.

Weiss, Harry B. *Life in New Jersey*. New Jersey Historical Series. Newark: D. Van Nostrand Company, 1964.

INDEX